Manufacturing the Gang

Recent Titles in
Contributions to the Study of Mass Media and Communications

The Press on Trial: Crimes and Trials as Media Events
Lloyd Chiasson Jr., editor

Personalities and Products: A Historical Perspective on Advertising in America
Edd Applegate

Taking Their Political Place: Journalists and the Making of an Occupation
Patricia L. Dooley

Developing Sanity in Human Affairs
Susan Presby Kodish and Robert P. Holston, editors

The Significance of the Printed Word in Early America: Colonists' Thoughts on the Role of the Press
Julie Hedgepeth Williams

Discovering Journalism
Warren G. Bovée

Covering McCarthyism: How the *Christian Science Monitor* Handled Joseph R. McCarthy, 1950–1954
Lawrence N. Strout

Sexual Rhetoric: Media Perspectives on Sexuality, Gender, and Identity
Meta G. Carstarphen and Susan C. Zavoina, editors

Voices in the Wilderness: Indigenous Australians and the News Media
Michael Meadows

Regulating the Future: Broadcasting Technology and Governmental Control
W.A. Kelly Huff

Native American Speakers of the Eastern Woodlands: Selected Speeches and Critical Analyses
Barbara Alice Mann, editor

Mass Media in 2025: Industries, Organizations, People, and Nations
Erwin K. Thomas and Brown H. Carpenter, editors

Manufacturing the Gang

Mexican American Youth Gangs on Local Television News

RAÚL DAMACIO TOVARES

Contributions to the Study of Mass Media and Communications, Number 63

GREENWOOD PRESS
Westport, Connecticut • London

Library of Congress Cataloging-in-Publication Data

Tovares, Raúl Damacio, 1952–
   Manufacturing the gang : Mexican American youth gangs on local television news / Raúl Damacio Tovares.
      p. cm. — (Contributions to the study of mass media and communications, ISSN 0732-4456 ; no. 63)
   Includes bibliographical references and index.
   ISBN 0-313-31827-1 (alk. paper)
   1. Mexican American criminals—Press coverage—United States. 2. Mexican American youth—Press coverage—United States. 3. Gangs—Press coverage—United States. 4. Television broadcasting of news—United States. I. Title. II. Series.
PN4888.H57T68   2002
070.4′4493643471073—dc21   2001040588

British Library Cataloguing in Publication Data is available.

Copyright © 2002 by Raúl Damacio Tovares

All rights reserved. No portion of this book may be reproduced, by any process or technique, without the express written consent of the publisher.

Library of Congress Catalog Card Number: 2001040588
ISBN: 0-313-31827-1
ISSN: 0732-4456

First published in 2002

Greenwood Press, 88 Post Road West, Westport, CT 06881
An imprint of Greenwood Publishing Group, Inc.
www.greenwood.com

Printed in the United States of America

The paper used in this book complies with the Permanent Paper Standard issued by the National Information Standards Organization (Z39.48-1984).

10 9 8 7 6 5 4 3 2 1

For Alla

Contents

Acknowledgments		ix
Chapter 1	Introduction	1
Chapter 2	Historical Roots of the Mexican American Youth Gang	31
Chapter 3	Influence of Newsworkers	61
Chapter 4	Police Influence	97
Chapter 5	Community Leaders	135
Chapter 6	Conclusion	163
Bibliography		169
Index		179

Acknowledgments

I would like to thank several persons for their help with this book. In its earlier phase, it was read by Federico Subervi-Vélez, John Downing, Sharon Strover, and Charles Ramirez-Berg all of the University of Texas at Austin, and Ricardo Romo, University of Texas at San Antonio. I am enormously grateful for their intellectual and moral support.

Many others helped me. Douglas Storey was the first person to hear about my idea to study Mexican American youth gangs on local television news and was very supportive. América Rodríguez provided some guidance and valuable references. August Grant introduced me to television station managers and news directors in Austin.

Chapters 1 and 2 were read by Lana Rakow and Jim Hikens at the School of Communication, University of North Dakota. Marwan Kraidy of American University and Félix Gutiérrez of the Freedom Forum also offered valuable comments and suggestions. Susan Craig and the Trinity College library staff helped track down several sources.

Financial support was provided by a Graduate Opportunity Grant from the University of Texas at Austin as well as summer research grants and a Moody Minority Doctoral Fellowship. I have also been assisted by a grant from the Radio Television News Directors Foundation and a fellowship from the Poynter Institute.

I am grateful to the journalists who shared their time and thoughts with me. They will no doubt see the shortcomings of this work since they know firsthand the complexity and richness that is found in local television news. I also want to thank the police officers, community leaders, and young people who gave me their time and insights. This work would not have been possible without their assistance.

I also want to thank my parents. I feel particularly blessed by their encouragement, for as long as I can remember, to express myself in whichever way I chose.

Thanks also go to Eric Levy and Lynn Zelem, my editor and production editor, respectively, at Greenwood, for their advice, patience, and help.

Finally, while I had much help writing this book I should say that any errors are mine and mine alone.

Chapter 1

Introduction

On September 19, 1990, two persons were shot and wounded in broad daylight near a bus stop in downtown Austin, Texas. Along with other news media, local television stations rushed production units to the scene. The incident was reported live by local television news as a gang shooting. Sixteen-year-old Bonifacio Alba was later charged with shooting and wounding sixty-one-year-old Tony Flores and a sixteen-year-old girl. Both were struck by bullets from a 9mm pistol. Another person, sixteen-year-old Roy Rios, was also wounded in the shooting, but Alba pleaded guilty only to wounding Flores and the teenage girl.

The shooting was a story that the news media could not overlook. It had occurred at the state capital, in the downtown area, as office workers were starting to head home. The shooting, according to news reports, had been the result of a feud between two rival "gangs."

Reporters at the scene of the shooting and anchors sitting behind news desks immediately began to report about gang involvement in the downtown shooting. The first television station to report the shooting told viewers that "At least one witness said the shooting occurred between two rival gangs. The witness said members of the two gangs began shooting each other" (September 19, 1990, 5:00 P.M. newscast).

At a competing station an anchor asked the reporter who was at the scene, "some of the witnesses, we understand, said that this was a gang related shooting. What have you heard?" The reporter replied that "right now police are still investigating that possibility although all of the witnesses that were there have told police that they believe all the members involved in this were gangs or members of gangs." The reporter went on to explain the reason witnesses told police that they believed gangs were involved: "Witnesses told police that they saw teenagers, maybe eight or nine, in front of a drugstore at Fifth and Congress. Then these other teenagers got off the city bus. At that time there was some taunting, and that's why one of the witnesses said he believes they were gang members" (September 19, 1990, 6:00 P.M. newscast). A third television station told viewers "Witnesses say two gangs began arguing then one of the gang members pulled a gun" (September 19, 1990, 6:00 P.M. newscast).

After years of reporting about a "gang problem" in Austin, the shooting at the corner of Fifth and Congress in the downtown area provided dramatic "proof" that the city was on the verge of being overrun by gangs.

Some police officers and community leaders made statements on live television about how they had been warning the city for years about the possibility of such an event. Austin, they said, could no longer afford to keep its head in the sand. The shooting at Fifth and Congress meant that Austin had an "emerging gang problem." The time had come when politicians and bureaucrats needed to face reality and deal with Austin's gangs. The shooting, many agreed, was a wake-up call for the community.

Immediately after the story about the shooting aired, angry residents began calling city hall to tell then Mayor Lee Cooke that if something wasn't done about the gang problem in Austin they would have to take the law into their own hands. Many threatened to start carrying firearms to protect themselves (Higginbotham, *The Daily Texan*, Sept. 21, 1990; Higginbotham, *The Daily Texan*, Oct. 1, 1990, p. 1). The day after the shooting, the mayor addressed the citizens of Austin at a press conference carried by local television news to ask that they remain calm. He assured Austinites that the gang problem was being addressed and under control. The incident led to the formation of the Mayor's Task Force on Crime, Drugs and Gangs, one month after the shooting (Haglund, 1991). The Austin Police Department announced increased patrols for the downtown area, especially along Fifth and Congress. The citizens were assured that there was no need for panic.

At the same news conference, Sgt. Harold Piatt of the Austin Police Department said that there was some question about whether the downtown shooting was gang related. It may have been caused by "wanna-bes," that is, persons who want to be members of gangs. Piatt also said that the incident may have been the work of one individual and not a gang (Higginbotham, Sept. 21, 1990, p. 1).

Three months later the *Austin American-Statesman* reported that Alba's attorney, Darwin McKee, said his client was not a member of a gang. McKee did say that his client did have close friends who were gang members and that "they may have been trying to get him to join" (Banta, Nov. 27, 1990, p. B1). Thus, what had originally been reported by local TV news, and other media, as a gang shooting may have been initiated by someone who did not belong to a gang. It was never reported whether the police had determined, after conducting a proper investigation, if anyone else at the corner of Fifth and Congress on that September afternoon had been members of gangs. In the absence of such an investigation, questions about gang involvement in the Fifth and Congress shooting would remain unanswered.

Not only did the shooting at Fifth and Congress lead to increased patrols in the downtown area, heightened anxiety about gangs taking over the city, and the creation of a citizens's task force to deal with problems associated with minority youths, it also led to an episode of the television series *Top Cops*. In this program, two officers of the Austin Police Department's Gang Unit were cast as hometown heroes trying to stop a "gang war." The highly exaggerated television program depicts two rival gangs in a shouting match. A brawl, which included highly choreographed martial arts moves, leads one of the gang members to pull a gun and begin firing indiscriminately. Several persons appear to have been fatally wounded. The episode ends when a teenager turns in his brother as the shooter. The television program made the two officers who were the focus of the *Top Cops* episode local celebrities.

The media coverage of the shooting at Fifth Street and Congress highlights many of the issues associated with news stories about gangs. A shooting in which minority youths are involved, in this case mostly Mexican American teenagers, is reported as a "gang shooting" or "gang-related" incident. The reaction on the part of some television news viewers was panic about the city being overrun by gangs. City leaders called for a study of crime, drugs, and gangs in an attempt to assure citizens that the problem was being addressed. The result was a list of recommendations that led to, among other things, the passage of a city-wide curfew for youths.

The reporting of the Fifth and Congress shooting in the summer of 1990 took place in the larger context of a state and nation experiencing a growing young, minority population, especially young Mexican Americans. The Latino population was and continues to be, numerically, the fastest growing minority group in the nation. At the same time, national economic policies in the 1970s, that had been a reaction to increased oil prices and the rise of the information age in the 1980s led to a widening of the gap between rich and poor. Increasingly, members of minority groups, especially the young, found themselves among the poorest of the poor. Under these conditions, policies that justified increased police surveillance of poor neighborhoods were instituted. How local television news contributed to this increased hysteria that led to increased police surveillance and other methods of social control directed at Mexican American youth is the focus of this book.

NEWS AS SOCIAL PROCESS

Understanding the portrayals of Mexican American youths on local television news rests on an appreciation of news production as a social process. By "social process," I mean that news stories are points of convergence where individuals, groups, and institutions struggle for control of the different discourses that influence the definition of social reality (Carey, 1992; Elliott, 1972; Hallin, 1994; Schudson, 1995; Turow, 1984; van Dijk, 1991). These discourses, or forms of expression that establish parameters for what is said and thought (Acland, 1995, p. 10), contain, among other things, the attitudes, beliefs, and biases constructed and maintained by the social, economic, and cultural systems. It is for this reason that the Mexican American youth gang news story is not a "true" or "objective" rendering of the experiences of Mexican American youths, nor can it ever be. Instead, the Mexican American youth gang story is like a magnet, attracting discourses that reinforce the existing social order and simultaneously casting to the margins of legitimate discourse competing interpretations of the Mexican American youth gang that threatens the power and privilege of the elite. In this sense, the Mexican American youth gang news story, like all news stories, is the result of the work of social actors—journalists, sources, and audiences—who are engaged in a tug-of-war over competing meanings (Gans, 1980, p. 81).

In this book, I critically examine how different social actors attempt to control the discourses influencing the production of the Mexican American youth gang story on local television news. I explore how this control comes to reflect dominant ideas, beliefs, and values in the form and content that have become journalistic clichés: the rising tide of violence; the spread of, and addiction to, more powerful drugs; and alienated minority youths. Such news stories assume the form and content that they do because such form and content serve a purpose. In very broad terms, that purpose is to contribute to the stability of society and further the interests of those in power. The discourse of Mexican American youths as members of criminal gangs contributes to that purpose in significant ways.

WHY STUDY LOCAL TV NEWS?

There are two important reasons for learning how local television news stories about Mexican American youth gangs are produced. The first is the development of local television news in the last few years. Since the late 1960s, television news has been transformed from a basic no-frills service to a flagship high-profit program. It has evolved from a bare-bones operation designed primarily to satisfy Federal Communications Commission (FCC) regulations that required broadcasters to provide the viewing public with information about their communities into a lucrative programming strategy that few television stations can afford to be without (Kaniss, 1991, p. 102). Currently, it is not uncommon for local television stations serving large metropolitan areas to produce several news programs per day. Many television viewers across the country have the choice of tuning-in to morning, noon, early afternoon (five o'clock, six o'clock) and late evening (ten o'clock) news programs. Such accessibility is accompanied by features unique to television news. For example, television news goes beyond the limitations of newspapers and radio in, among other things, its capacity to transmit both sound and video messages into virtually every home in a television market. The pervasiveness of local television news highlights the importance of studying how it presents groups and individuals to the viewing public.

A second reason for studying the portrayal of Mexican American youths on local television news is the demographics associated with this segment of the population. Because the Mexican American community is relatively young, media representations of this group apply to a large number of persons. Moreover, this segment of the population is expected to grow at an increasing rate in the near future. Social programs, however well-intentioned, that are driven more by exaggerations and distortions rather than more balanced and accurate portrayals of Mexican American youths may aggravate the problems already related to this group, such as high levels of incarceration. For example, one researcher found that in the late 1980s, just prior to the shooting in downtown Austin, approximately 1,890 juveniles were being referred to the Texas Youth Commission every year. Of the 1,890 juveniles, 28.4 percent were white, 28.9 percent were black, and 42.5 percent were Hispanic (Iscoe, 1990, p. 80). Weich and Angulo (2000) found that nationally "Over-representation of minority youths in the juvenile justice system increases after arrest" (p. 38). They also report that in Texas "in 1996, minority youths represented 80 percent of those juveniles held in secure facilities, while representing only 50 percent of the overall state juvenile population" (p. 39).

All of this is not to say that the Mexican American youth gang exists only in television news. Field work and discussions with community leaders made it clear that indeed there are Mexican American youth gangs. Some of the members of these gangs do engage in criminal activity. However, some evidence indicates that the overwhelming majority of Mexican American youths will never join a gang, and of those who do, most will not become involved in criminal activity (Buhmann, 1992). In addition, the characteristics associated with youth gangs, including those made up mostly of Mexican Americans, are typically negative. Positive characteristics found by researchers of Mexican American youth groups are ignored by the news media. Indeed, the news media report on youth gangs as a social scourge that must be eliminated. In the public mind, youth gangs are associated with violent initiation rites, drug addiction, and drive-by shootings, to name only the three most salient associations. Rarely is the youth gang reported as a support group that can give an individual a sense of self-esteem and reinforce ethnic identity, yet some researchers have found this to be the case (Moore, 1991; Vigil, 1988, esp. Chap. 3). Vigil, who studied Mexican American youth gangs in California, reported that these gangs "play a significant role in helping mainly troubled youth acquire a sense of importance, self-esteem, and self-identity" (p. 64).

One purpose in writing this book is to explain the apparent discrepancies between television news reports about Mexican American youth gangs and the findings of researchers who have studied them. For example, television news, like print media, tends to report about a growing gang problem. Yet researchers have found that the number of adolescents and young men who join gangs has remained stable over many years. Another discrepancy is found with respect to increased violence. While access to automatic weapons has become easier, most Mexican American young people, including those who are part of a gang, do not engage in violent behavior. A third discrepancy is with the relationship of the Mexican American gang to the family. While some gang members may come from troubled homes, many Mexican American adolescents who live in troubled homes will never join a gang, and some of those who live in stable, two-parent families may engage in criminal activity. Such discrepancies indicate that there may be something more going on in the production of the Mexican American youth gang stories than merely reporting the "facts." If such is the case, then there is a need to identify the influences on the Mexican American youth gang stories on local television news. In addition to identifying such influences, we need to understand how these influences operate in the process of local television news production to give us the stories about Mexican American youth gangs that appear on living room TV screens.

MEDIA REPRESENTATION

The study of how Mexican American youths are portrayed on local television news is related to how youths in general and members of minority groups are presented by the news media. Some researchers have found that news stories about young people and minority group members tend to be greatly exaggerated (Cohen, 1972; Falchikov, 1986; Hall et al., 1978; Males, 1999). By selecting the most sensational and dramatic stories and allowing recognized authority figures, such as the police, to provide interpretations of events involving young members of minority groups, news reports can be slanted to favor mainstream stereotypes and prejudices. A consistent pattern of such reporting, in conjunction with the absence of more favorable reports, can serve to reinforce stereotypical images about young minority group members (Turner & Surace, 1956; Zatz, 1987). Current portrayals on local television news of Mexican American youths as violent drug abusers unable or unwilling to conform to society's rules can lead to policy decisions that may exacerbate problems in the community. Incarceration, increased police surveillance, arrests, unreasonable searches, and suspicion of an individual because he happens to be young and Mexican American can lead to feelings of frustration and resentment among this segment of the population. At a time when relations between Anglo Americans and people of color, including Mexican Americans, appear to be tense, such negative portrayals of Mexican American youths can only aggravate the situation. The backlash against affirmative action, immigration policies, and the English First movement are three examples of how such tension manifests itself.

Although studies have not determined what, if any, effects the news media have on individuals or society, some researchers believe that under certain conditions news portrayals may reinforce stereotypical thinking about minority groups. For example, Hartman and Husband (1974) found that when individuals lacked direct interaction with members of minority groups, there was a greater tendency to accept portrayals of those groups as presented by the news media. In the United States, a large number of ethnic groups have come to identify themselves as "Americans." However, differences in class, customs, language, and religion persist. Often we learn about persons in our own communities, especially those different from ourselves, through the media, including the news media. Thus the information gained from local television news contributes to the formulation of ideas, attitudes, and perceptions about persons who are different from us. For this reason, information that constructs a group as "a growing problem," "out of control," and "a threat to the community," as youth gangs usually are, can have detrimental consequences for the group in question and the entire community, if such a construction is based on skewed data, exaggerations, and myopic vision.

In a society that appears to be increasingly divided into affluent and poor groups, especially among young people (Sum & Fogg, 1991), opportunities for interaction among different groups such as affluent Anglos and poor Mexican Americans may decrease. Inner-city neighborhoods are geographical areas more affluent citizens know they should avoid. With the rise in number of "gated communities" and the privatization of public spaces and services, we can expect decreased interaction among social classes. As a result of such a decrease, portrayals of Mexican American youths presented on local television news may become more believable to affluent viewers who lack opportunities to meet and interact with Mexican American youths but have opportunities to sit on committees, commissions, and advisory boards where decisions that affect the lives of Mexican American youths are often made (Dorfman & Schiraldi, 2001, pp. 5, 29).

That local television news stories about Mexican American youth gangs are biased should not be interpreted to mean that there is no violence among young people in Mexican American nieghborhoods. Nor should this lead to the conclusion that all reporting of drug use in Mexican American neighborhoods is a fabrication. Rather, recognizing that news stories about Mexican American youth gangs reflect dominant values and beliefs should make us aware of how ethnicity and age influence news stories about Mexican American youths. As a result facile conclusions based on stereotypical thinking and prejudicial beliefs are communicated to viewers through stories that leave the assumptions underlying such thinking and beliefs unquestioned.

Problems of violence and drugs in Mexican American neighborhoods do exist. However, when such stories about Mexican American youths are reported, there is a tendency to introduce the "gang" discourse and present this phenomenon as "normal" behavior associated with the neighborhood. When similar stories about predominantly white, suburban middle-class youths are reported by the media, the tendency is to explain such behavior as an anomaly.

For example, in San Diego, California, eight teenagers, who were described as "good boys," were fighting a new California law that allows prosecutors instead of judges to decide whether to try a juvenile as an adult. According to a story in *USA Today* (Alvord, 2000, p. 4A), the boys, all white except for one, admitted to using pellet guns to shoot and beat five migrant workers, all of whom were over the age of sixty. Because of the passage of Proposition 21 in California, prosecutors now have the authority to decide whether to try a juvenile as an adult. Previously, judges made such decisions. Lawyers for the teenagers argued that their clients were not receiving due process. The parents of the boys said that their sons were being treated too harshly. These boys drove from their homes to labor fields looking specifically for Latinos to shoot, attack, and rob. One man was beaten so badly that the boys thought they had killed him. The teens were described as above-average students. Some were athletes at a public high school attended by students from the surrounding affluent neighborhoods.

In Littleton, Colorado, the infamous Columbine shootings were carried out by two teenagers who attended Columbine High School. The two students belonged to an organization known as the Trench Coat Mafia. Several students belonged to this group. On April 20, 1999, two students killed twelve students and one teacher before they killed themselves. While the term "gang" did occasionally come up in magazine stories and reports about the shooting, it was more likely that the word "clique" would appear. The teenagers who opened fire on their classmates spoke openly with each other about killing students. They posted messages alluding to killing on Web sites. They wore similar clothing. Newspaper articles about the killings, like the one that appeared in the *Atlanta Journal and Constitution* (April 21, 1999, p. 1A), failed to mention the word "gang" in the story. Witnesses, parents, and others interviewed for the articles may have mentioned the word "gang" in their description of the Trench Coat Mafia, but officials never used the term.

The *Washington Post* reported about the murder of a member of a Northern Virginia drug ring over a deal gone bad. The young men involved, two were twenty-one and the other twenty, had been supplying drugs to several friends and acquaintances. One of the members of the drug ring, according to the article, frequently supplied $100,000 worth of marijuana, along with other drugs, to his associates who would sell the marijuana for a profit and pay back the $100,000. However, Daniel Petrole was taking the marijuana and not paying back. He was shot to death with a 9mm semiautomatic pistol outside his house by one of the members of the ring. The *Post* article noted that the investigation of the murder of Petrole "uncovered one of the most significant drug operations in the region's history. The killing has led [the police] to an extensive network of suburban teenagers and young men who sell high-grade marijuana and ecstasy to thousands of customers throughout Northern Virginia—most of them still in high school" (White, 2001). The drug ring consisted of white, suburban, affluent teenagers and young adults. The murder victim's father had been with the Secret Service and his mother was a school teacher at the time of the shooting. The word "gang" never appears in the 2,723-word story.

These examples indicate how the application of the term "gang" is selective. While affluent teens in suburbs who get into trouble with the law are seen as individuals who may have made a mistake because of their youth and inexperience, poor minority youths who make the same mistakes are more likely to be seen as part of a "gang," and their troubles with the law are more likely to be interpreted as a problem rooted in the family, social conditions, or cultural shortcomings.

CRITICAL PERSPECTIVE

A critical view of the Mexican American youth gang discourse presented on local television news reveals that the basic assumptions on which such discourse rests are rarely questioned. When such questions are raised, many of the arguments for a proactive stance against the Mexican American youth gang problem begin to unravel. Answers to a simple question, such as "what constitutes a gang?" can unveil a scene of, at best, naive optimism, at worst, racism and deceit. What is referred to as gang activity in one setting, among young people from a resource-poor social class and in a particular geographic space, such as an ethnic neighborhood, may be dismissed in an upper-class, suburban setting as a youthful indiscretion. For example, after records were stolen from a fraternity house on the Colgate College campus, revealing organized, systematic, illegal behavior sanctioned by the group, including gang rapes, drinking and drug use, and the promotion of racist and sexist attitudes, associate professor of sociology Rhonda Levine stated, "If these were working-class kids or poor kids in an inner-city ghetto, we'd call them a gang and we'd call them pathological" (Warshaw, 1989, p. 207).

In Austin, Texas, the mother of a fraternity pledge who was being initiated into the organization reported finding her son hiding in a closet, his legs and buttocks covered with bruises. In an affidavit the woman claimed that her son had been beaten with a broomstick, walked on by persons wearing boots, and led around by a cloth wrapped around his testicles ("29 Fraternities," 1990, p. 26L). The term "gang" never came up in the newspaper report.

Such discrepancies between stories about Mexican American and white middle class youths allegedly involved in criminal behavior indicate a need for a closer look at Mexican American youth gang stories on local television news. Going behind the superficial reporting about "gang" activity can reveal how the process of production leaves myths about Mexican American youths untouched.

Critical examination of the Mexican American youth gang discourse on local television news allows for the development of different perspectives on this social phenomenon. Rather than relying on unquestioned assumptions as springboards for studies about Mexican American youth gangs, critical theory requires that such assumptions be examined for evidence of how the social system is reified in the production of local television news. An understanding of the Mexican American youth gang stories for local television news from a critical perspective also opens the possibility for challenging the stereotypes perpetuated in such reports.

CRITICAL THEORY

Critical theory can be traced back to the works of Marx, Gramsci (1971), Althusser (1971), Horkheimer and Adorno (1994), Marcuse (1964), and Habermas (1991), among others. A key element running through the works of these theorists is that inherent in the process of communication is a struggle for power over the definition of social events (van Dijk, 1993). Such power manifests itself in economic, social, and cultural strategies. Ignoring or denying the role of power in the communication process leads to a distorted view of social interaction. Yet power is difficult to define.

Persons who control large amounts of capital are said to have economic power. Others who may control resources by virtue of their elected or appointed status as heads of city, state, or national governments or agencies are said to have political power. Still others may be able to influence cultural processes because of their artistic talent and/or prestige within the artistic community. Others may have power in the sense that they can resist attempts by those with economic, social, and cultural power to control their behavior. In the process of news production, different persons and organizations use their power to influence how social reality is defined (Gans, 1980, pp. 332–333).

Critical theory argues that communication is the manifestation of our thoughts and beliefs about ourselves and our relationship to others. It focuses on what human beings make of their social experiences in order to discover how we should act and live (Hallin, 1994, p. 18). Explaining why we act and think the way we do reveals how behavior and beliefs are often the result of the tension of both arbitrary decisions and immediate solutions to practical problems as well as the products of a long, historical process.

Within critical theory, Gramsci's (1971) work on how ideology and institutions contribute to the stability of society is especially helpful when studying the Mexican American youth gang story on local television news. A primary question guiding Gramsci's work is how power is exercised in the modern, liberal, democratic state (Kellner, 1990, p. 17). Specifically, it is concerned with how the elite maintain their rule, or hegemony, without resorting, except in extreme cases, to physical violence. A significant element in this aspect of the theory of hegemony is the role played by the mass media, especially the news media, in the manufacturing of a consensus that supports the prevailing ideology and the interests of the ruling elite while simultaneously appealing to a broad segment of the audience in order to maintain their legitimacy and in this way contribute to hegemonic rule.

A main tenet of Gramsci's (1971) work is that the stability of society is closely tied to the prevailing attitudes, beliefs, and ideas, or what in Marxist terms would be referred to as ideology. However, for Gramsci, the term "ideology" does not carry the same weight that it does in Marxist theory. While still important, because it sets limits and provides direction for changing attitudes, beliefs, and ideas, ideology does not *dictate* people's attitudes, beliefs, and ideas. Like Marxist theory, ideology for Gramsci encompasses a world view that rests largely on unspoken assumptions. The result of this world view is a system of social values that, in the process of communication, are seamlessly incorporated into everyday living and come to be accepted as "common sense." This "common sense," a form of rhetoric, serves to reaffirm those in power by organizing thought and behavior around the interests of the dominant classes (Fiske, 1989, p. 169). Thus the power to control discourses about what is right and wrong, acceptable and unacceptable, legal and illegal occurs in an economic, legal, and social setting, in which different groups attempt to define events to their best advantage. The economics of what McManus (1994) refers to as "market-driven journalism" and the poverty in which many Mexican American teenagers find themselves both contribute to hysteria about Mexican American youth gangs. In the legal setting, the police, courts, and detention centers contribute to the Mexican American youth gang discourse by offering views on the extent of the problem, its possible causes, and solutions. Finally, a society with a racist past that has convinced itself that racism is a thing of the past offers a social setting in which Mexican American youths can be treated differently from other youths. The decision to treat young Mexican Americans defined as drug-addicted violent criminals differently is based on "common sense," including the idea that, because racism has been eliminated, such treatment must be "color-blind."

According to Gramsci's theory of hegemony, government makes up only one part of the system of power. Institutions and organizations that also accept the prevailing ideology and incorporate it into their everyday operations make up the other parts of the system. The family, the church, political organizations, unions, and the mass media all support the prevailing attitudes, beliefs, and ideas through their organizational structures, programs, and activities. These institutions, organizations, and associations serve as a secondary line of defense should the core institutions, such as the government, banking system, or social system, find themselves weakened or delegitimized (Femia, 1981, p. 191).

The mass media, because they are among the major institutions in advanced capitalist societies, have a political function in that they too promote the dominant ideology (Femia, 1981, p. 27; Kellner, 1990; van Dijk, 1987, pp. 40–46). This dominant ideology, which permeates every aspect of an organization, shapes production including cultural products like news stories. In this way, the prevailing ideas of a time and place are "seamlessly" incorporated into the news stories that are presented as "objective" and "fair" and most important, "natural." In fact there is nothing natural about Mexican American youth gang news stories. They are the result of economic, social, and cultural struggles to define social events.

News organizations, then, can be said to mediate the views of dominant groups as well as those of the subordinate groups. This is why news stories can be described as points of convergence reflecting different discourses. However, those discourses are the result of access to resources such as money, people, and technology. Persons and organizations with access to resources such as money, people, and technology have an advantage when articulating and promoting a point of view (Gandy, 1982). Funds, for example, can be used by large institutions to hire professionals to write press releases and then distribute those releases through the mail, fax machines, and the Internet. Spokespersons can be briefed and made available for news segments and talk shows. Prepared statements can be written with television news formats in mind. Such strategies can tilt the balance of power about how to define and discuss an issue or topic against those persons and organizations that do not have access to such resources.

It must be kept in mind that the news media, like other institutions, have to maintain their legitimacy in the eyes of the public, and so their role is not solely to maintain the social order. Indeed, there may be times when the need for legitimacy conflicts with their role as promoters of a point of view associated with a government body or elite institution. In this sense, the role of the news media goes beyond merely promoting social stability, as a functionalist interpretation of the role of the mass media in society would argue (De Fleur & Ball-Rockeach, 1989, esp. chap. 5, pp. 123-142).

Gramsci recognized that ideologies are not written in stone. As different groups struggle for power over the definition and interpretation of reality, the dominant ideas, values, and beliefs may shift to accommodate these challenges and promote social stability (Hebdige, 1979, pp. 15-19). This flexibility is a key factor in the rise and stability of the modern liberal state. As new groups ascend the economic and social ladder, they are able to redefine their experiences and forge new identities that are more beneficial to their members in terms of social status and prestige. With respect to news stories about Mexican American youth gangs, different groups attempt to influence the production of these stories in order to, consciously or unconsciously, promote their varied interests in the public sphere.

A major weakness of Gramsci's theory of hegemony is the definition of hegemony itself. Gramsci failed to provide an exact description of how people come to accept the prevailing ideas of the time and decide to go along, to give their consent, to be governed. According to Femia (1981, p. 24), hegemony is the result of the various ways that institutions can shape the cognitive and affective states through which persons perceive and assess social experience. At the center of this process is the economic system because it organizes the system of rewards that is used to discipline various members of society for the benefit of the elite. The legal system is also crucial because it defines acceptable and unacceptable behavior in the business and social spheres.

But it is important to note that for Gramsci, the routines imposed by the economic and legal system need not lead to blind conformity. Indeed, the irony of routines is that they can make possible an escape from the grip of ideology and even lead to nonconformist thinking (Femia, 1981, pp. 30-31). Thus, one strength of the concept of hegemony is that it goes beyond mechanistic and Marxist approaches to the study of mass media in society; however, it fails to make explicit how some people can come to a critical assessment of their secondary status and force changes in the economic and legal institutions that can lead to the improvement of their economic and social conditions.

As mentioned, the concept of "common sense" is the result of various factors, including historical material. The theory of hegemony recognizes that the past does influence the future. However, Gramsci's view goes beyond historical determinism, which argues that people are slaves to the past. Nor did Gramsci believe that history is an endless cycle of recurring events. Such an approach fails to address how the past can influence the present. Gramsci believed that, while the past does impose limitations on our thinking, it is also possible to see beyond those limitations and begin to formulate alternative futures from the perspective of the subordinate (Gramsci, 1971; pp. 344–346). Understanding history and relating it to the commonsense thinking of the present can help us become more conscious of how we came to define youth gangs and associate them with Mexican American youths. Of course, gangs are also associated with African American and Asian American youths. The histories of those associations are well worth researching, and no doubt similarities between the Mexican American and African American and Asian American youth gangs exist. Much of the popular literature on gangs focuses on African American young men. Many studies indicate that African Americans are targeted for harassment and arrest, experience racial profiling, and receive harsher prison sentences than whites or Latinos (Weich & Angulo, 2000; Mauer, 1999). More recently, Asian teenagers and young adults have come to be associated in the news media with gangs. The tradition of samurai, tongs, and other such groups fuels the public's fear of Asian crime. The relationship of these ethnic groups to local television news certainly deserves closer study; however, in this book, I focus on the Mexican American youth gang because it is the phenomenon I studied and with which I am most familiar.

A BRIEF HISTORY OF THE MEXICAN AMERICAN YOUTH GANG

The history of Mexican American stereotypes can be traced back to the opening of the Santa Fe Trail in 1821 (Wilson and Gutiérrez, 1995; p. 65). Competition for control of this lucrative trade route led to tensions and, in some cases, violent confrontations between Europeans and Mexicans. The Battle of the Alamo in 1836 was another significant event in the stereotyping of Mexicans. The image of the Mexican as a blood-thirsty savage, with General Santa Anna serving as an icon for the Mexican people, was crystallized during this period of conflict between the United States and Mexico. The war with Mexico occurred between 1846 and 1848 and further served to stereotype Mexicans. Through narratives presented in pulp fiction, and later silent films, these images remained part of the popular perception of Mexicans (Pettit, 1980). In the late 1800s and early 1900s, because of political turmoil in Mexico, increased immigration and urbanization led to large concentrations of Mexicans in major U.S. metropolitan centers, the most important of which was Los Angeles.

By the 1920s, researchers such as Bogardus (1926) in Los Angeles and Thrasher (1942) in Chicago were already investigating "Mexican boy gangs." In the 1930s, there was much concern about the growing problem of Mexican youth gangs expressed in the pages of the *Los Angeles Times*. By the 1940s, such concern had developed into full-blown hysteria that manifested itself in what have come to be called the "zoot-suit" riots in 1943, during which military personnel stationed near Los Angeles began to randomly beat young Mexican American males. According to Turner and Surace (1956) the zoot-suiter was unambiguously labeled in the press as a negative symbol in order to create a distinction between zoot-suiters and Mexicans. The zoot-suit riots remain a defining moment in the history of the Mexican American youth gang. One reason for this is that it represents the first time that modern news organizations, the *Los Angeles Times*, the Hearst-owned *Examiner*, and the *Herald-Express*, reported extensively on this young segment of the Mexican American population.

Studies have shown that at each of these periods in history, the media's concern with the problem of Mexican crime and gangs was overblown (Domer, 1955; Mazón, 1984; Paredes, 1973; Pettit, 1980). The popular press is traced back to the 1830s with the origination of the "penny press" of Benjamin Day, the same decade when Samuel Morse developed the telegraph. In time, advertising dollars would overtake subscriptions as primary sources of income for newspapers. Such a change meant that consumers of news stories were themselves being sold to advertisers by newspaper publishers. Stories became important as a way to attract an audience for the ads placed alongside news copy (Potter, 1954, pp. 179–182).

The introduction of broadcast radio in the 1920s further intensified the need to attract audiences. This pattern would repeat itself in the late 1960s and early 1970s when television stations would find that local television news could be profitable. Such political, economic, and social changes influenced how news was defined and produced. It is within this context that the origins of the Mexican American youth gang story for local television news need to be studied.

MEXICAN AMERICAN YOUTH GANGS AND THE NEWS MEDIA

There are several perspectives on how the Mexican American youth gang is portrayed by the news media. Some of these perspectives posit an all-powerful news media that can dictate how people think and act. Others offer explanations based on sociological theories about the news media. Still others look at cultural factors and ethnic differences to explain how the Mexican American youth gang is distorted by the news media. But all these perspectives, to some extent, fail to examine the basic assumptions that underlie the Mexican American youth gang story and their relationship to the social structure. This failure largely explains why the Mexican American youth gang discourse has remained well within narrowly defined themes like the problems of violence, drugs, parental apathy, and community disorganization.

The "all-powerful media" perspective argues that Mexican American youth gangs were fabricated by the police and the news media. McWilliams (1990) dismissed the Mexican American gangs of East Los Angeles in the 1940s as inventions of the police and the press. He notes how relatively minor incidents involving Mexican teenagers and young adults were played up by the newspapers and the police in the spring of 1942 "to build up, within a short period of six months, sufficient anti-Mexican sentiment to prepare the community for a full-scale offensive against the Mexican minority" (p. 206). For example, McWilliams notes that a fight between two groups of Mexican American youths in the summer of 1943 was reported by the press as a fight between the Belvedere "gang" and the Palo Verde "gang." He also mentions that in all of these reports about gang fights the ethnicity of the boys involved was never overlooked (pp. 206–207). Indeed, McWilliams wryly points out that in Los Angeles in 1942, the saying "boys will be boys" had been revised to "boys, if Mexican, will be gangsters" (p. 216).

Gonzales (1981) also attributes the creation of the Mexican American youth gang to exaggerations in the press, which were supplied by the police. Writing about the early part of 1942, when the Los Angeles Police Department and the Los Angeles press were focusing on and dramatizing delinquency in Mexican neighborhoods, Gonzales notes:

> This period can be seen as the time during which the "gang" image was developed and "marketed." During this time the Los Angeles community was being informed as to the extent and nature of these "gangs."

Thus, the "gangs" were *created* and *defined*. (p. 136. Emphasis in original)

Such "powerful effects" or "hypodermic needle" models of mass communication have been dismissed by communications scholars for failing to explain how social groups have often resisted and rejected media messages (Hall et al., 1975; Fiske, 1989). These "powerful effects" models assume a passive audience lulled by messages transmitted by a monolithic system of mass communication that is controlled by a homogeneous ruling elite. The explanatory power of such a model leaves much to be desired when we consider that Mexican American agricultural workers, for example, rejected the stereotype of themselves as "stoop laborers" and organized for improved working conditions (Meier & Rivera, 1972, pp. 238–239). Also, many Mexican American high school students in the 1960s and 1970s, despite being labeled "culturally deprived" and in some cases even "mentally retarded," challenged those labels and demanded classes that would improve their chances of securing a college diploma rather than accept being "tracked" into vocational classes (Macias, 1970). While it would be foolish to deny that the mass media have some power to influence audiences, examples like the ones just cited indicate that it would be equally foolish to attribute absolute power to the mass media.

Another perspective on Mexican American youth gangs and the news media accepts the existence of Mexican American youth gangs but questions how these are used to promote stereotypes about Mexican American youths. Turner and Surace (1956) found that late in the ten-year period studied, the *Los Angeles Times* came to associate the term "zoot suit" with Mexican American youth gangs. They argue that the word "Mexican" had too many positive associations for the people of Los Angeles. Such positive associations about Mexican culture would not have allowed Los Angeles residents to react violently to Mexican youths said to be members of gangs. However, by referring to these youth gangs as "zoot suiters," the *Los Angeles Times* was able to whip readers into a frenzy that led to several days of attacks on Mexican American youths. What is striking about Turner and Surace's study is how the discourse about Mexican youth was altered to "zoot-suit" crime as an unambiguous symbol that triggered a negative stereotype that facilitated the unleashing of the community's and the military's fears and anxieties. While they are careful to note that questions about the effects of the mass media are far from settled, Turner and Surace's approach also rests, albeit tacitly, on a powerful effects model of the mass media. Granted, theirs is a "softer" version of the one described by McWilliams (1990) and Gonzales (1981), and therein lies the strength of their argument. Turner and Surace move away from the theory that the media created gangs to one that begins to examine the interaction between the mass media (in this case newspapers) and readers and the social environment.

Relying more on a cultural model of how the news media interact with other social forces is the work of Zatz (1987). She explores one southwestern U.S. city's reaction to a perceived threat from Mexican American youth gangs. Her analysis of the gang phenomenon in Phoenix, Arizona, in the 1980s led her to conclude that "it was the social imagery of Chicano youth gangs, rather than their actual behavior, that lay at the root of the gang problem in Phoenix" (p. 153). Zatz points out, based on quantitative and qualitative data gathered from Juvenile Court referrals, that gangs and gang-related crimes were a reality. However, contrary to the reaction to gang-related crime, the police did not organize special units to deal with regular street crime, corporate crime, and other types of illegal activity. She notes in her study of court referrals in Tucson, Arizona, that those Chicanos believed to be members of gangs were mostly guilty of having been involved in "minor squabbles." Only one referral out of 518 "gang boys" was for a non-fighting violent crime.

> Contrary to the impression given by the police that gang members were "armed and vicious" . . . it appears that gang boys typically engaged in relatively minor squabbles, and not in murder, rape or serious violent crimes. (p. 140)

The imagery of gangs as violent converged with that of Mexicans as "different" to facilitate the police and news media's promotion of a moral panic (see Cohen, 1972). Identifying Mexican American youths as responsible for community disorder paved the way for an increase in the number of social control agents in Mexican American neighborhoods (Zatz, 1987, p. 154).

What is not clear in Zatz's (1987) study is exactly what role ethnicity played in the creation of the moral panic about Mexican American youth gangs in Phoenix and Tucson. Moral panics related to youth have been created in societies much more homogeneous than many of the U.S. communities that are currently said to be experiencing gang problems. In many cases, social class differences, rather than ethnic differences, seem to serve as a basis for the creation of a moral panic about youth gangs (see Pearson, 1983, for a study of "hooliganism" in Great Britain; Cohen, 1972; and Hebdige, 1979). This should not be interpreted as a denial of the role that ethnicity plays in the gang discourse but rather as recognition that the role of ethnicity in this phenomenon and how it interacts with other factors, such as social class, proportion of the ethnic population, immigration patterns, and quality and quantity of media coverage, is far from settled. In the pages that follow, I will show how an understanding of the Mexican American youth gang news story is related to the interests and duties of several sources such as reporters, the police, community workers, and young people themselves. These interests are reflected in the Mexican American news stories we have come to accept as part of the almost daily diet of information delivered by newspapers, radio talk shows, and local television news.

METHOD

The method for studying the Mexican American youth gang on local television news in Austin, Texas, consisted of interviews with police officers, newsworkers, and community leaders, as well as young people, some of whom claimed to be members of gangs. These categories were not necessarily exclusive. For example, some community leaders active in antigang campaigns admitted to having been members of gangs as teenagers. In some cases, community leaders were adolescents involved with social service agencies that encourage primarily young Mexican Americans to stay away from gang violence and drugs.

Critical study of a social phenomenon such as youth gangs requires a qualitative approach. Qualitative methods are more open-ended and exploratory than the more structured and formal quantitative methods. Qualitative researchers are driven by general questions that guide, rather than limit, their investigation. They also recognize that the researcher is part of the research process. That is, the mere presence of a researcher investigating the production of news stories about Mexican American youth gangs may alter the context in which such stories are produced. Qualitative approaches, then, can be described as more flexible than quantitative approaches.

In contrast to qualitative methods, quantitative approaches begin with specific hypotheses and well-defined terms. Studies are designed to collect data that are used to either support or reject the hypotheses noted at the beginning of the study. The definitions used in studies of gangs are often so narrow as to make the data based on them worthless. Often researchers ignore their own methodological assumptions and proceed to conduct research without a clear definition of a gang. Inherent in research based on quantitative methods is a belief in objectivity and a clear distinction between the researcher and the research. The quantitative researcher assumes a clear division between observation and participation. Such bifurcation of the research process, a Western European concept, is questioned by qualitative researchers.

Another assumption on the part of quantitative researchers is the quantification of social phenomenon. Data that result from counting the number of gangs and gang members or number of stories on local television news about gangs are used to draw conclusions about the gang problem and, consequently, offer solutions. Qualitative researchers argue that such data, based on narrowly defined terms, obscure rather than clarify the phenomenon being studied. In this sense, they merely re-create the social prejudices and stereotypes they claim to be investigating and helping to alleviate.

Qualitative researchers, on the other hand, claim that social phenomena are too complex to be reduced to a set of numbers that can be statistically analyzed and reduced to an F ratio and a probability value. In the process of communication, too many unknown variables influence how human beings may react to information. These unknown variables, qualitative researchers argue, make the prediction and control of human behavior promised by quantitative methods impossible.

Like all studies in the social sciences, the terms and phrases used in this work present a thorny problem. What exactly is a "Mexican American youth gang"? The words "Mexican," "American," "youth," and "gang" can take on a variety of meanings.

Jankowski (1991) explains how the word "gang" was applied to adult criminals in the late 1800s and early 1900s. Adults involved in organized crime were said to belong to gangs and were called gangsters (Jankowski, 1991, p. 2 and Introduction). Ausbury's (1970) *The Gangs of New York*, first published in 1927, deals almost exclusively with adult criminals. In the 1920s, after Thrasher (1942) published his study of youth gangs, the word "gang" became associated with groups of juvenile delinquents, although Thrasher used the terms "gang" and "mob" interchangeably. Later "syndicate" came to signify those groups involved in organized criminal activities (see Jankowski, 1991).

In this book, the term "Mexican American" will refer to persons of Mexican ancestry who are residing in the United States. Again, this is not as simple as it sounds. One community leader who considers herself a "Chicana," a term associated with more progressive Mexican Americans, has a distinctly English last name. A witness who appeared on camera to provide an account of a shooting in a neighborhood said to have a gang problem is named Sandra Robles. Ms. Robles spoke with a distinct East Texas accent, had blonde hair, and very light skin. Her children, shown in the television report, had dark hair and skin darker than their mother's. The term "Chicano" is also problematic for research purposes. Although it has a long history (see Mazón, 1984), the word "Chicano," an abbreviation for "Mexicano," came to be used in the second half of the twentieth century as a way to distinguish persons of Mexican ancestry who were born north of the U.S. Mexican border (Gómez-Quiñones, 1990, p. 7). In the first half of the twentieth century, the word "Chicano" had some pejorative connotations (Meier & Rivera, 1972, p. xiv). Many older Mexican Americans never felt comfortable with the term. Today, there are still many Mexican Americans who refuse to refer to themselves as Chicano or Chicana. While many, but by no means all, older Mexican Americans are uncomfortable with the term, some younger ones, again by no means all, reject it as well (see Meier in McWilliams, 1990, p. 304).

Even the word "youth" poses problems for the researcher. A youth in one place or time may not be defined as such in another place or time. Platt (1977) and Ariés (1962) have addressed this problem. Even in our own society and time, the definition of the word "youth" can change depending on the circumstances. For example, in most states someone under the age of twenty-one is considered too young to purchase and consume alcohol, while someone under the age of seventeen who is accused of murder may be tried as an adult. Sum and Fogg (1991) have noted "the lengthening of the transition from adolescence to economic adulthood in American society" (p. 88). In the 1950s, most teenagers in the United States could expect to find a job, marry, and raise a family soon after graduating from high school. Earning wages comparable to those of adults was a right of passage of sorts into the adult world. Because of this earning power, many eighteen- and nineteen-year-olds were considered adults. But by 1988, Black and Hispanic young men were earning 54% of the median income of adult males employed full-time. This steady decline in the earnings of many young men, especially Blacks and Hispanics, argue Sum and Fogg, in addition to a 29% decrease in their real weekly wages since 1973, makes it difficult to recognize this population as full-fledged adults. A teenager may be defined chronologically as someone between the ages of twelve and twenty. But defining an adolescent or "youth" is more problematic. Age, economic status, and opportunities to assume the duties and obligations associated with being an adult all add to the complexity of tackling such a definition.

Another problem in defining the Mexican American youth gang is related to how television news departments convey information about incidents involving Mexican American youths who commit crimes. Some newspapers, radio, and television news departments have agreed not to mention the names of gangs or gang members in their stories (Gang Unit Officer, personal communication). One of the recommendations made by the *1992 Texas Attorney General's Gang Report* is that press coverage not sensationalize gang-related behavior (Buhmann, 1992, pp. 28 and 34). In addition, youths arrested for involvement in criminal activity usually do not have their names mentioned on the air (Stephens, 1993, p. 431). How then can a television news story be categorized as a "Mexican American youth gang story"?

There is a perception held by many viewers of local television news in the southwestern United States that many Mexican American youths are involved in gangs. However, in the absence of explicit identification by nationality or ethnicity by the news media of persons who are reported to be involved in illegal or deviant activities, how are Mexican American youth gangs identified by viewers? What cues or other forms of identification of the Mexican American youth gang have been introduced? Although this book does not analyze the effects of the Mexican American youth gang story on the viewers of local television, it cannot ignore the cues within Mexican American youth gang stories that may contribute to the perception of Mexican American neighborhoods as being ridden with gangs. These perceptions about Mexican American youth can spill over into other forms of television programming. For example, in a popular television game show that depends on word associations, one contestant gave the clue "They have a lot of these in East L.A." To which his partner immediately responded "gangs" (Cortés, 1993, p. 3).

Since the late 1960s and early 1970s, the news media have been encouraged not to identify alleged criminals by ethnicity. *The Associated Press Broadcast News Handbook* (1982) notes that identification by race should occur only when in a biographical sketch in which the appointment of a member of a minority group represents a break from routine appointments; when the viewer or listener, in the case of radio, will enhance his understanding of an issue by knowing the race or ethnic group of those involved; when describing someone sought in a manhunt (p. 236). More specifically, with respect to crime stories, Stephens (1993) notes that:

> A suspect's race or ethnic background should not be mentioned unless it is connected to the motivation for the crime or unless the suspect is still at large and, as part of a detailed description, it may aid in the arrest. (p. 261)

The use of video in television news, of course, helps, in some cases, circumvent the policy of not mentioning the ethnicity of teenagers believed to be involved in criminal activities. Skin color can indicate the ethnicity of Mexican American teenagers alleged to be members of gangs. In addition, other clues can tip-off the viewer about the ethnicity of someone accused of committing a criminal act. Viewers are commonly told by the anchor in which neighborhood, block, or intersection an event being reported took place. In addition, in the opening or "establishing shot" of a story, viewers can see in which neighborhood the activity being reported occurred and they can surmise the ethnicity of many of the residents who live in that part of town. Street names also provide information about the area in which an incident that is being reported took place and, in general, the ethnicity of the persons who live there. Warr (1994) notes that there are strong indications that crime is perceived in geographic terms (p. 15). Graffiti on walls, abandoned buildings, and dilapidated housing all serve as cues of dangerous places that should be avoided.

Last names, especially in the case of Mexican Americans who tend to have Spanish surnames, of victims and those arrested can also lead to associations between crime and ethnicity. Finally, video, even when not showing the adolescent's face, can establish the ethnicity of the person arrested. Skin color, clothes, and the surroundings in which the arrest takes place all can contribute clues as to the ethnic identity of the person arrested. The association of crime, neighborhood, and ethnicity can create a powerful symbol that is interpreted as a threat by the viewer of local television news.

Caution on the part of the researcher, however, is in order. Because someone is arrested in a particular part of town, such as a *barrio*, should not lead to the assumption that that person is Mexican American. Even being Spanish surnamed is not a guarantee of being of Mexican descent. According to the 1990 Census, Travis County, Texas, in which most of the research for this book took place, had a population of 576,407, of which 120,049 were persons of "Hispanic Origin." Of this total, 106,722 were classified as Mexican, 1,710 as Puerto Rican, and 703 as Cuban. In addition, 10,914 were classified as "Other Hispanic." However, there is a higher concentration of minorities in the city than there is in the county. That is, more minorities live in the city than in the surrounding communities. While 21.1% of the residents of Travis County, which includes the city of Austin, were Hispanic, 23% of the city residents were Hispanic (U.S. Bureau of the Census, 1990).

While attempting to formulate precise definitions for purposes of research is important, perhaps equally important is the acknowledgment that the terms and phrases used in studies such as this one are often ambiguous. This is because the same term, such as "gang," is dependent on shared cultural values for common understandings. For example, when the sportscaster of a television news team states that "the gang here in the sports department will bring you those scores as soon as they are available," viewers understand that the "gang" is different from one that is reported in the sentence "The gangs in this neighborhood are indicative of a much bigger problem." It should not be overlooked that ambiguous meanings can give words more power. The perceptions of the viewer can dismiss the "gang" of the first example as harmless while interpreting the "gang" of the second example as a threat to the public order. Such associations can become very strong. For example, studies have shown that in controlled experiments subjects shown pictures of crimes, such as robberies, assaults, and murders, will tend to associate the criminal with African American or some other minority group even when visual cues indicate that the perpetrator is white. Many researchers have found a close association in the public's mind between crime and minority status.

In the study of the Mexican American youth gang on local television news, it is important to recognize that such flexibility in the use of terms and phrases lends itself to ambiguity about the subject matter. This ambiguity can contribute to the exaggerations about the presence of Mexican American youth gangs in the community. Rather than assuming that one's definitions are all encompassing and accurate, it is best to take a more reserved approach and proceed cautiously, always with the thought in mind that one's definitions are far from exact.

In addition to the problems associated with the definitions of terms, the study of an ethnic group in the United States also tends to introduce unfamiliar terms. Some familiarity with these terms will be helpful. In the Mexican American community, gang members are sometimes referred to as *pachucos*. Although I did not hear the word very often in my interviews with leaders of the community, it is not uncommon to run across it in the literature (see Moore, 1978; Sánchez, 1943; Vigil, 1988). Another term for one who exhibits the Mexican American youth gang style of dress is *cholo*. Still another term that is important in the history of the Mexican American teenager, and Mexican American community, is the term "zoot suit."

The zoot-suit style of dress, popular in the late 1930s and 1940s, consisted of baggy pants, long-tailed coats, wide-brimmed hats, and high boots. Ducktail haircuts and ankle-length watch chains were also part of the style (McLemore & Romo, 1985, p. 19; also see Mazón, 1984, for a detailed study of the zoot-suit riots).

Between April 1993 and January 1995, a total of twenty-seven persons in Austin were formally interviewed for this study about Mexican American youth gangs and their representation on local television news. Among the twenty-seven informants were twelve newsworkers, nine community leaders, and six police officers. Among the newsworkers were three news directors, one general manager, and three anchors. Several television news reporters were also interviewed. Community leaders included a priest, neighborhood organization representatives, activists, parents, and social program directors or community program directors. Among the six police officers interviewed were current and former members of the Police Department Gang Unit, and patrol officers.

All interviews were recorded on microcassette when permission was given by the informants and the conditions allowed for such recordings. Interviews in offices, living rooms, and classrooms were not a problem in terms of audio recording. However, some situations made audio recordings impossible. For example, during the "ride-along" with one police officer, no recordings were made. The length of the "ride-along," an entire eight-hour night shift, the ambient sounds, and almost constant radio communication would have made such a recording inaudible. Also, when interviewing some members of an organization dedicated to preventing gang violence by using young people as role models, I was asked by the director not to record the very young members of the organization to protect their privacy. Interviews were loosely structured. So long as the topic of gangs and the media remained the general focus, no attempt was made to force the interviewees to agree or disagree with prepared statements or comments.

The survey approach was rejected in favor of an open-ended, more exploratory approach.

As a Mexican American male studying the production of the Mexican American youth gang story for local television news, I was aware that my presence might influence discussions at news production meetings, the assigning and coverage of stories, and the content of interviews. It may have also influenced how the community leaders and young Mexican Americans I interviewed responded to my questions. On the one hand, white newsworkers and informants may have assumed that as a Mexican American I would automatically take an adversary role vis-à-vis the news media. Mexican American community leaders, on the other hand, may have assumed that as an academic I would promote the values and beliefs generally found in the reports of middle-class researchers, reporters, anchors, and producers. In addition to these two extremes, there were many variations in the interactions between myself and sources, as the chapters that follow demonstrate.

Local television news stories about gangs that aired in the television market were also examined. Access to these stories was facilitated by permission from the three network-affiliated news stations to observe the television news production process firsthand. In addition to interviewing newsworkers, I sat in during production meetings, went out into the field with crews producing general news stories and some stories on gangs, sat with reporters in editing suites while they edited their stories, and sat at adjacent desks while they researched stories. At one of the stations, VHS copies of locally produced gang stories were made available. I also searched for stories on databases at two of the stations and then screened the stories at the city's archive of local television news housed at the Austin History Center.

In the following chapters, I apply this method to explore, from a Gramscian perspective, the influences on the Mexican American youth gang story for local television news. In Chapter 2, I review the history of the Mexican American youth gang to better understand how past reporting about the Mexican community is related to current television news stories about this social group. In Chapter 3, I examine how the news production process influences reporters' perceptions of the Mexican American community and Mexican American teenagers. How reporters are trained to produce stories, who they select as sources, and the pressures under which they work all have an impact on the television news Mexican American youth gang story. Chapter 4 is dedicated to the role of the police in molding news stories about

Mexican American youth gangs. As symbols of the "thin blue line" that separates law and order from chaos and collapse, the police can influence the content of Mexican American youth gang stories. In Chapter 5, the Mexican American community, specifically its leaders and activists, is studied to find out how these citizens contribute to the image of Mexican American youth gangs on local television news. Parents, teachers, community organizers, program directors, and teenagers all attempt to put their own spin on Mexican American youth gang stories. The last chapter summarizes the major points of this study and includes some strategies for combating superficial and harmful images of the Mexican American community and Mexican American youth perpetuated by local television news.

This book should contribute to an expansion of the Mexican American youth gang discourse. By making available information about the process within which the Mexican American youth gang discourse on local television news is contextualized, I hope to stimulate discussion about this phenomenon that goes beyond clichéd thinking or common sense and worn out phrases. Understanding the Mexican American youth gang story as social process allows us to see beyond the narrow frames within which such stories are presented. Such narrow frames can be both explained and broadened to include both questions about the Mexican American youth gang that help broaden the field of vision within which it is presented on local television news and in this way problematize the Mexican American youth gang story on local television news.

Chapter 2
Historical Roots of the Mexican American Youth Gang

> Friday night, before the posse left the ranch, they endeavored to wring from the younger [he was thirteen] of the robber's boys information concerning the plans of the three who escaped. The boy refused to talk. He was hung up to a tree until his tongue protruded and life was nearly extinct, but he steadfastly declined to reveal any of the secrets of the gang.
> (*S.A. Express*, June 16, 1901, p. 1 cited in Paredes, 1973, p. 71).

The origins of the study of the Mexican American youth gang are typically traced to the 1920s and the work of Emory Bogardus (1926) in California (Moore, 1978, p. 42; Vigil, 1988, p. 6). Bogardus studied the problems of what he referred to as "boy gangs" in Los Angeles and in his *City Boy and His Problems* (1926) made several references to "Mexican boy gangs" (pp. 86, 93, 104, and twice in 107). While there can be no doubt that Bogardus's work marks the origins of twentieth century scholarly interest in Mexican American youth gangs, taking Bogardus's work as a point of departure ignores a rich and complex period of history that influenced the work of Bogardus and other researchers of Mexican American youth gangs who followed.

This chapter argues that the origins of the representation of the Mexican American youth gang on local television news are actually rooted in the social, political, and economic conflicts of the 1800s. While the work of Bogardus (1926) helps us understand many of the perceptions of Mexican American youth gangs that are common today, the tensions and conflicts of the 1800s between Mexicans and Anglos, or whites, in the western and southwestern part of what is now the United States helps us understand the perceptions of the Mexican boy gangs held by researchers in the first half of the twentieth century. Such perceptions found expression in the representation of Mexicans and Mexican Americans in newspapers and pulp fiction in the 1800s. Woll (1980), who studied the images of Latinos in film, notes that while Hispanics in general were stereotyped as evil by the media of the 1800s, Mexicans in particular were stereotyped as not only violent but barbaric (p. 54). Examining the coverage of Mexican "bandit gangs" by the media in the 1800s helps develop an appreciation for the richness of the history of the Mexican American youth gang story on local television news.

A primary reason for misunderstandings, distortions, and stereotypes about Mexican American youth gangs, and consequently of the Mexican American community, is that the news media, including television news, typically present these groups as an ahistorical phenomenon. This is nothing new, indeed, an argument could be made that ahistoricism is part of the history of the modern Mexican American youth gang story. But of course, Mexican American youth gang news stories aired by local television news in the 1980s and 1990s did develop within a historical context. Like all social phenomena, the portrayal of the Mexican American youth gang by the news media in the 1980s and 1990s is related to past events that continue to influence the production of these stories. This portrayal developed from a long history of social tensions and hostilities related to ethnic, political, economic, social, and cultural factors. Some of the more salient factors include the competition over control of trade routes in the early 1800s, wars between Mexico and the United States, ethnic clashes on Mexican and U.S. territories, the development of Progressive and Nativist thinking, increased immigration, and the rapid urbanization that occurred at the turn of the twentieth century.

Most important, for the purposes of this book, is the development of mass media during the 1800s. Understanding local television's portrayal of the Mexican American youth gang in the latter part of the twentieth century requires some knowledge of events that preceded such coverage. More importantly, understanding the history of the Mexican American youth gang as it is presented by local television news allows us to examine not only how the present is related to the past but also how alternative futures may be developed. By alternative futures is meant other possibilities of how to live and work that are the result of an understanding of the past and a self-awareness based on that understanding as opposed to clichéd thinking that is simply a conditioned reaction to past events.

GRAMSCI AND THE STUDY OF HISTORY

Within Gramscian theory, history is seen as a means for understanding the present and, based on that understanding, developing strategies that can lead to positive changes in the future. However, it is important to keep in mind that such alternative futures must themselves be grounded in the past. The importance of studying history is that it allows us to understand that the present is not "natural" or "normal" but the result of choices made within an environment influenced by the interplay of political, economic, cultural, and technological forces. By understanding how those forces contributed to the way we live today, the way we think and interact with one another, and therefore contribute to a definition of the present, we can come to realize that the future can be modified in such a way that it will improve living conditions.

Stating that people are not immune to the forces of history is not the equivalent of stating that they are slaves to the past. Gramsci believed that by understanding history, people can come to realize that their everyday lives are the products of choices made in the past, which in turn influence the choices being made in the present. Without an awareness and understanding of the influence of history on our thinking, our decisions only tend to reinforce stereotypical thinking, or common sense, and in this way contribute to the hegemonic order.

However, by consciously analyzing the present in terms of the past, we can come to understand how social phenomena are cultural artifacts reflecting the way we live. That is, the choices based on political, economic, and cultural factors are manifested in the artifacts and practices of our everyday lives. One of those artifacts is the local television news story. Alleviating the problems associated with, or exacerbated by, Mexican American youth gang stories on local television news—stereotyping, gross oversimplification, ethnic and generational tensions—requires an understanding of how these stories developed and then strategizing to change such stories, or eliminating them altogether, by first challenging and later altering beliefs, ideas, and values associated with this kind of reporting. Thus, we study the history of the Mexican American youth gang story on local television news in order to understand how it developed and based on that understanding strategize for altering it in the future in such a way that it will benefit Mexican American youths, the larger Mexican American community, and the news media.

EARLY HISTORY

The portrayal of the Mexican American youth gang on local television news can be traced back to ethnic tensions and conflicts going back to the early 1800s. These tensions and conflicts are related to patterns of immigration and urbanization, which in turn are related to economic and political factors. Within this broad context the introduction of drugs, and their association with the Mexican American youth gang, is important. Drug control legislation, specifically the Marijuana Tax Act of 1937, demonstrates that social policy changes can be the result of and lead to an intensification of negative feelings toward a minority group. Changes in social policy can and do affect how Mexican American youths are perceived. Throughout the twentieth century, the demonization of some drugs has had a great influence on the public's perception of Mexican Americans in general and Mexican youths in particular (Barker, 1974, p. 21; Becker, 1963, p. 135).

The history of the news media and its representation of these economic, social, and political tensions and conflicts are key factors in our understanding of the Mexican American youth gang story in today's local newscasts. While local television news is a relatively recent phenomenon, the production of news stories about Mexican "gangs" is well over 100 years old. These stories evolved as a result of an increasingly literate society, economies of scale, and improved systems for processing and distributing news and information. An examination of that system of mass-produced news and information helps us understand the television news stories about Mexican American youth gangs on television news in the 1980s and 1990s.

GROWTH OF LITERACY AND RISE OF PRINT MEDIA

In the late 1800s newspapers and popular fiction were, for the first time in history, reaching a mass audience. There are three primary reasons for this growth in readership. The first is that literacy rates in the United States began to increase with the development of the public school system. Massachusetts, and the rest of New England, established the first public schools, called common schools, starting in the 1820s (Schultz, 1973, p. 69). Soon other states followed suit. As public education systems continued to be funded by state governments, more people learned to read. Public education, therefore, was an important factor in creating an audience of readers.

The second reason for the establishment of a literate society is that printing technology improved the speed and efficiency with which books and newspapers were produced. In September 1833, Benjamin Day started *The New York Sun*, the first of the "penny papers," so called because they were affordable to the "common man." The penny papers were ideal for bringing advertisers seeking to sell goods and services together with a growing community of readers willing to pay for them.

Finally, the development of the first electronic system of communication, the telegraph, cannot be overlooked in a study of the growth of the mass media. While certainly not the cause for the mass publication of newspapers, the telegraph did spur the growth of the penny papers (see Schudson, 1978, pp. 31–35). Equally as important is that the telegraph facilitated the growth of economic activity. The first telegraph line between Washington, D.C., and Baltimore was established in 1844. By 1846, the Mexican War was being reported by newspapers still dependent on the pony express, steamboats, and railroads. However, a fledgling telegraph "system" had been added to these other systems of communication (Emery et al., 1996, p. 116).

The Mexican War was the first foreign war covered by American reporters (Emery et al., 1996, p. 116). Although there were arguments made against the war with Mexico, the penny papers overwhelmingly lent it their support. In addition to supporting the U.S. government these newspaper reports about the war with Mexico also supported the idea of Manifest Destiny, the term given to the philosophy that divine providence had ordained the settlement of the west by Anglo Americans (Emery et al., 1996, p. 117). News reports about the war with Mexico served to promote the war-hero images of military leaders like Zachary Taylor and Winfield Scott and mirrored the distrust and prejudices against Mexicans which many Anglo Americans held at the time (Emery et al., 1996, p. 117).

Other less dramatic, but also important, developments in the production of news were occurring during the 1800s. Flat presses were replaced with rotary presses that could print both sides of a roll of paper simultaneously, thus increasing production to meet the growing demand for newspapers. The combination of the rotary press, also known as the Hoe cylinder press, with the steam engine meant further reduction in the production cost of each paper. Books, like newspapers, could also be mass produced using this new technological innovation. These developments are also important to the understanding of the growth of pulp fiction, which carried many of the stereotypes associated with Mexican Americans in the 1800s and early 1900s (Pettit, 1980).

Mass-produced newspapers and books mean little without the capacity to reach a larger number of people. Improved postal and railway systems were making possible the distribution of these mass-produced books to new markets. Thus, by the mid-1800s, the basic elements of a system for gathering and distributing news and information were in place.

However, printing presses and telegraph systems alone do not determine the content of news. Content is determined by systems of production and distribution in conjunction with political and cultural factors. Again, the media play a significant, but not a determinant, role in this process. Some of these political and cultural influences on the coverage of the early Mexican bandit gang news stories are important to the understanding of the Mexican American youth gang story on local television news.

ROOTS OF TENSIONS AND CONFLICTS BETWEEN MEXICANS AND ANGLOS

As mentioned earlier, some researchers trace Mexican and Mexican American stereotypes as far back as the opening of the Santa Fe Trail in 1821 (Wilson & Gutiérrez, 1995, pp. 65–67). Native people had used this route long before Anglo traders began to haul goods from Independence, Missouri, to Santa Fe, New Mexico. In the early 1800s, however, competition between Anglos and Mexicans for control of this lucrative route led to a heightening of tensions between these two groups. Differences in political systems, culture, and religion contributed to the mutual feelings of suspicion and distrust both groups had for each other.

Mexico declared its independence from Spain in 1821, the same year that the Santa Fe Trail opened. The distance from the capital, Mexico City, and the financial burdens incurred while fighting for independence meant that the northern provinces were given low priority by the Mexican government. In addition, the harsh desert terrain of northern Mexico made this geographic region difficult to control. In the early 1800s, indigenous peoples still controlled much of the area of what is now the southwestern United States.

Providing goods to the people of Santa Fe was seen as an economic opportunity by some enterprising Americans. This entrepreneurial spirit also reinforced the philosophy of Manifest Destiny. William Bucknell, a small businessman from Franklin, Missouri, went down the Santa Fe Trail in 1821 and returned a year later with leather bags filled with silver. His success motivated others to trade with the Mexican city to the south. By 1830, *The Missouri Intelligencer*, the first frontier newspaper established west of St. Louis, was informing its readers about the rapidly growing trade between the United States and Mexico:

> This is perhaps one of the most curious species of foreign intercourse which the ingenuity of American traders ever originated. The extent of country which the caravans traverse, the long journeys they have to make, the rivers and morasses to cross, the prairies, the forests and all but African deserts to penetrate, require the most steel-formed constitutions and the most energetic minds. (Duffus, 1930, p. 108)

As stated earlier, what is today the southwestern United States had been traversed by Native Americans and others long before U.S. traders began using it to transport goods. However, the idea of physically and mentally strong "American" traders opening the Santa Fe Trail is closely tied to the ideology of Manifest Destiny. Such a philosophy expressed itself not only in the need to trade for profit and control trade routes, but also in the arrogant, brash, and sometimes boorish behavior on the part of some of the Anglo traders. There were Anglo Americans who had married into Mexican families and settled in the Santa Fe community. But increased trade and immigration from the United States, as well as attempts by the U.S. government to buy Mexico's northern territories, led to increased tensions between Mexicans and Anglos.

Abuses on the part of Mexican government officials also contributed to tensions and conflicts. For example, in the late 1820s, Governor Manuel Armijo confiscated the goods of a young trapper named Ewing Young. Among the most lucrative items of trade at that time were beaver furs. Accompanying Ewing Young was Milton Sublette, who took his share of the furs and, after hiding for some time in Santa Fe, left for the United States. Governor Armijo threatened the American community in Santa Fe if it did not turn Sublette over to him. Sublette escaped from the town and then made it across the border into the United States—with his furs (Gregg, 1966, pp. 227–229). The lack of cooperation on the part of the Anglo community heightened Armijo's suspicion about the loyalty of these new Mexican citizens.

Such incidents served to dramatize the tensions resulting from unfair tariffs. Often trappers were told by Mexican officials to pay up to 100% in taxes in order to get furs out of the country and into the United States. If unable or unwilling to pay, furs could be confiscated and the trappers jailed. This kind of treatment led to outrage on the part of American trappers and sympathy from their countrymen living in Santa Fe.

Religion was another source of tension (Pettit, 1980, p. 7). The Protestant Americans viewed themselves as independent thinkers who had broken free of European religious traditions. They saw Mexicans as dominated by a corrupt clergy under the control of the pope. Gregg (1966), who traveled into Mexico between 1833 and 1836, wrote about his travels in the region. One chapter, Chapter 8, is dedicated to the Catholic religion in Mexico and its influence on the population. The chapter opens with the following:

> The Mexicans seem the legitimate descendents of the subjects of "His Most Catholic Majesty," for the Romish faith is not only the religion established by law, but the only one tolerated by the constitution: a system of republican liberty wholly incomprehensible to the independent and tolerant spirits of the United States. (p. 172)

Equally perplexed, however, were Mexican officials who could not understand how men who spoke of freedom for all insisted on bringing slaves to the northern provinces. Such religious differences could not be settled without a disruption of the lifestyle, beliefs, and culture of one group.

When the Mexican government abolished slavery in 1829, whites from southern slave states who had settled in what was then northern Mexico felt politically betrayed and economically threatened. The following year the Mexican government, alarmed at the increase of Anglo settlers occupying lands in its northern province, passed the Decree of April 6, 1830, which prohibited further immigration from the United States (Moquin, Van Doren, & Rivera, 1971, p. 162). Such restrictions resulted from legitimate concerns on the part of Mexican officials about how best to protect their northern borderlands. The general suspicion among Mexican government and military leaders was that Anglo settlers did not seem as loyal to their new country, Mexico, as they did to their old one, the United States.

The result of the war for Texas independence, especially the Battle of the Alamo in 1836, the Mexican War (1846–1848), and the annexation of Mexican territories into the United States, was a new social order. After the Mexican War, Texas assumed control of the Santa Fe-Chihuahua trade route (Montejano, 1987, p. 19). These actions further exacerbated the tensions and anxieties Mexicans and Anglos were experiencing.

In 1838, two years after the Battle of the Alamo and eight years before Texas joined the United States, Anthony Ganilh published *Mexico vs. Texas* in which he argued that it was the "divine duty" of Anglos to conquer Mexico and all of Latin America (Pettit, 1980, p. 22). Such writing promoted the philosophy that Northern Europeans had a God-given mandate to own and rule the entire Western Hemisphere.

While, in general, Mexicans who had lived in what is today Texas came under Anglo rule after 1836, the older and new elite families learned to share political, economic, and social power. Montejano (1987) describes how this new social order allowed the Anglo victors to maintain political control of what had previously been Mexican communities without the constant use of force (p. 34). But this did not mean that tensions did not exist between Anglos and Mexicans. Throughout the late 1800s, there were events that brought to the surface the bitter feelings harbored by both Mexicans and Anglos as a result of the military battles that led to the establishment of what at first was the independent nation of Texas and ten years later, in 1846, the state of Texas.

In 1857, Texas experienced the "Cart Wars," a series of battles for control of the trade route between Goliad and San Antonio. In the summer and fall of that year, masked bandits attacked and killed

Mexican traders as they traveled this route. Montejano (1987) points out that despite seventy-five murders, the authorities ignored demands from the Mexican community for action to stop the killings. No arrests were made and the result of turning a blind eye to the murders was that Mexican traders lost access to the frieght business conducted between San Antionio and the Gulf Coast (p. 29).

Two years after the Cart Wars, in 1859, Juan Nepomuceno Cortina led a "revolt" in South Texas. Legend has it that Cortina, born in 1824, was the son of a wealthy family whose land had orginally been granted by the Spanish Crown. Seeing Brownsville Marshal Bob Shears beat one of his, Cortina's, former ranch hands, Cortina shot Shears in the arm and took the drunken ranch hand to his *Rancho del Carmen*. Cortina was soon charged with attempted murder. He argued that he had shot Shears in self-defense, but the Anglo community leaders would not accept his claim. The result was the invasion and capture of Brownsville, Texas, by Cortina and his supporters. Cortina held the Brownsville region by defeating the local militia, the Brownsville Rifles, and an outfit from San Antonio, Tobin's Rangers. He was finally defeated by U.S. Army troops in December 1859 (Montejano, 1987, pp. 32–33). The ability to organize a band of men capable of defeating local authorities must have fueled fears in the local Anglo population about the Mexican community's ability to not only defend itself but to take over and control the community.

Ten years later, in 1869, the "second Cortina War" (Montejano, 1987, p. 53) started as a result of lowered beef prices. While the cost of beef declined, the value of hides increased. This economic change led to "skinning" raids and counterraids on both sides of the border. The targets of these raids were initially mavericks, or cattle that had no brand. Arguments about the rightful ownership of mavericks caused both Mexicans and Anglos to seize cattle. Anglos in South Texas organized vigilante raids that drove Mexican families out of their farms and then fenced those farms and claimed them as their own. One group of Anglos from Corpus Christi rode into the Upper Nueces area to ranches owned by Mexicans where they proceeded to kill every adult male in sight and burn ranch buildings. It was not until 1876 that the Texas Rangers had the problem of Mexican skinning raids and Anglo vigilantism under control (Montejano, 1987, p. 53).

Studying these conflicts in the state of Texas and understanding them from two different social, political, and cultural perspectives, Mexican and Anglo, provides a context that allows for a deeper appreciation of the development of ethnic stereotypes of which the

Mexican American youth gang is one of the latest. Differences in religious beliefs, political ideas, and cultural expressions provided material that, within an economic development context, served as sources of tension and conflict.

The mass media of the late 1800s, newspapers and pulp fiction, did not ignore incidents such as the Cortina revolt or other conflicts between Mexicans and Anglos. These forms of mass communication exploited this theme to attract an audience and sell product. In his study of the images of Mexicans in popular fiction, Pettit (1980) writes that the stereotype of the Mexican as lazy, cowardly, and vicious was promoted in "conquest fiction" that appeared soon after the Texas War for Independence (p. 22). But it was the publishing house of Beadle and Adams that provided the first novels about Spanish gentlemen who "may be well-bred dons of the range who lead double lives as public-spirited cattlemen and private leaders of bandit gangs" (p. 36). The examples cited above served as the basis for the idea of Mexicans banding together to form gangs engaged in activity outside the law. This was a strongly held belief in popular culture and one that could easily make the transition from pulp fiction to news stories, as the following case illustrates.

THE CORTEZ "GANG"

Perhaps the most famous Mexican "outlaw" in Texas at the turn of the twentieth century was Gregorio Cortez. In 1901, Cortez shot and killed Sheriff Morris after a misunderstanding over the trading of a horse. Sheriff W.T. (Brack) Morris did not speak Spanish and was depending on an interpreter whose Spanish was apparently less than fluent. In Spanish, a male horse is a *caballo*, while a mare is a *yegua*. Gregorio Cortez had traded a mare and when asked if he had traded a *caballo* replied that he had not. When Morris attempted to arrest Cortez, his brother stepped between him and the sheriff. The sheriff then shot Cortez's brother. Cortez returned fire, consequently killing Morris. A posse was organized and the *San Antonio Express* reported that it was looking for the "Cortez gang" (Paredes, 1973, p. 71). A few days later, the posse attempted to learn the whereabouts of the "Cortez gang" by hanging a thirteen-year-old Mexican boy until he was near death.

> Friday night, before the posse left the ranch, they endeavored to wring from the younger [he was thirteen] of the robber's boys information

concerning the plans of the three who escaped. The boy refused to talk. He was hung up to a tree until his tongue protruded and life was nearly extinct, but he steadfastly declined to reveal any of the secrets of the gang. (*S. A. Express*, June 16, 1901, p. 1, cited in Paredes, 1973, p. 71)

The boy's refusal to cooperate only proved to the members of the posse how determined the members of Cortez's "gang" were. In dealing with such obstinate persons, the use of extreme measures could be justified.

Newspapers along the border repeatedly wrote about the "Cortez gang" and played up the role of the Texas Rangers in the pursuit of Gregorio Cortez. Initial stories reporting on the chase were later found to be highly exaggerated. For example, on the property of Martín Robledo, officers told reporters that they had found an "arsenal" consisting of ten Winchester rifles and a lard bucket of cartridges. Two days later, the number of Winchesters found on Robledo's property was reduced to eight. A month later it was reported that only one Winchester and a shotgun had been found—an "arsenal" found in most homes in the area at that time (Paredes, 1973, p. 72).

In July 1913, after he had served time for the murder of Morris, Cortez was pardoned by Governor O.B. Coquitt. The pardon came as a result of several factors. Notable were the efforts of Colonel F.A. Chapa, the editor of *El Imparcial*, and a friend of Governor Coquitt. However, Paredes (1973) states that it was Gregorio Cortez's personality and the feeling that his sentence had been unjust that convinced people around him to appeal to the governor to grant a pardon. Among those who wrote letters of support of a pardon for Cortez were the prison chaplin, the warden, and the chief clerk of the Huntsville prison (pp. 97–98).

NEW MEDIA, OLD STORIES

Hollywood was quick to adapt the Mexican stereotypes found in newspapers and pulp fiction to the new medium of film as the release in 1911 of *Tony the Greaser* demonstrates. This film was followed by *Broncho Billy and the Greaser* (1914) and *The Greaser's Revenge* (1914) (Woll, 1980, p. 55). The defining characteristics of the "greaser" were his thirst for blood, excessive greed, and a blatant disregard for social values (Woll, 1980, p. 55). In *A Cowboy's Baby* (1910), the Mexican character throws the hero's child into a river. In *Western Child's*

Heroism (1912), the Mexican character attacks the Anglo Americans who earlier in the film had saved his life (Woll, 1980, p. 55).

There were, of course, other portrayals of "greasers." In some films, the Mexican character gains the good graces of the Anglo characters by turning against members of his own ethnic group and siding with the Anglo characters. In one film, *Tony the Greaser*, Tony saves the Anglo landowner's daughter. As a reward, Tony is permitted to kiss the daughter's handkerchief just before he dies (Woll, 1980, p. 55). Such "positive" portrayals, however, were rare. Most Mexicans in films were portrayed as bloodthirsty and uncivilized.

The portrayal of the Mexican Revolution on film also promoted images of Mexicans as prone to senseless violence. The Mutual Film Corporation produced *Barbarous Mexico* in 1913 and sent cinematographers to Mexico to shoot footage of revolutionaries like Pancho Villa. In fact, Pancho Villa had an exclusive contract with Mutual Film. The money he earned from this deal was used to buy arms in the United States (Clendenen, 1972).

These psuedodocumentaries, which would evolve into newsreels on which television news is modeled, became standard features of the movie-going experience in the early 1900s. Black and white film footage of the Mexican revolution was screened in theaters across the United States. The scenes of the rebellion in Mexico emphasized conflict and ignored underlying causes, such as economic factors and social justice issues. In the United States, the newsreel stories of the revolt that led to the downfall of Porfirio Díaz, who had ruled Mexico for more than thirty years, were ahistoricized. Such newsreel footage exhibited in U.S. movie theaters aroused anxiety and apprehension about Mexican mobs just south of the border who seemed to be rebelling for no apparent reason (Clendenen, 1972).

These films and newsreels were produced and presented within a social context that included discourses about the "foreign born," meaning persons from Latin America, Southern and Eastern Europe, and Asia and their ability to assimilate into "American culture." Theories developed in Europe by Cesare Lombroso about the relationship between race and crime reinforced stereotypical portrayals of Mexicans in the mass media. These theories reinforced the nativist movement in the United States. As old technologies were improved and new ones introduced, as the economy changed from an agricultural base to an industrial base, and immigration increased, the stereotypes about Mexicans, rooted in the tensions and conflicts of the 1800s, did not suddenly disappear. Instead, they themselves were undergoing changes. Such changes would allow for their reintroduction to society as new and different phenomena requiring new and different methods of social control.

ORIGINS OF THE STUDY OF THE MODERN MEXICAN AMERICAN YOUTH GANG

By the 1920s, with increased immigration and urbanization, concern about gangs shifted from "well-bred dons" who may have led double lives and barbaric "greasers" to city youths, who may have been "foreign" or been influenced by "foreign elements." Emory Bogardus (1926) in California and Frederick Thrasher (1942) in Chicago included Mexican gangs in their studies of boy gangs. Both researchers were influenced by the Progressive philosophy of the previous decades. Such a philosophy was reform-oriented in some respects, reactionary in others. For example, during the Progressive Era, activists like Jane Addams argued for proactive strategies to help the nation's youth, especially those with foreign-born parents. The basis of her work was rooted in the social disorganization theory of crime. Like many progressives, Addams believed that the decline or collapse of social institutions in the modern world led to disharmony within the adolescent, thus creating an individual inclined toward crime and deviance. Reinforcing social institutions, progressives argued, could lead to the grounding of the individual in middle-class values and lifestyles that led to social harmony. Rather than a critique of the social system as a possible source for delinquency, Addams and other social reformers of her time called for the strengthening of social institutions. Far from being a call for the radical alteration of social institutions, such an approach reaffirmed the faith that many progressives had in the economic, social, and cultural institutions of the time (Platt, 1977, p. 97).

The "child saver movement" was based on the assumption that a well-financed elite, which included such advocates as Jane Addams and Louise de Koven Bowen, could fund programs managed by middle-class professionals to create environments in which children would be able to blossom into productive citizens (Platt, 1977). There was no question in the minds of these reformers that the lifestyle of the American middle and upper classes was the cause for spiritual and physical well-being. Jane Addams, for example, although sympathetic to the plight of children in a modern industrial society, "remained within the bounds of orthodox political action" (Platt, 1977, pp. 97–98). The child saver and progressive movements dovetailed with the more liberal wing of the nativist movement.

The nativist movement in the late 1800s and early 1900s rested on the belief that the lifestyle and culture Northern Europeans had established in the new world was threatened by what were believed to be the less intelligent and less cultivated peoples from Latin America, Africa, Asia, and Southern and Eastern Europe. At one end of the nativist philosophy were those who believed that the culture and lifestyle of the Northern Europeans in the United States were the result of biology. Based on distortions of Darwinian evolutionary theory, many scientists argued that natural selection had blessed Northern Europeans with superior genes. For this reason, efforts to improve the education, training, or other opportunities for persons who could not trace their ancestry to Northern Europe were seen as a waste of money, time, and effort. Instead, tighter restrictions on immigration, based on country of origin and social class, were seen as the reasonable approach to the "problem" of miscegenation.

At the other end of the nativist argument were those who believed that, while the Northern European culture and lifestyle deserved to be protected and strengthened, through education, training, and other opportunities those outside of Northern European culture and tastes could learn how to become Northern Europeans. The flaw in both approaches is the privileging of Northern European culture and the denial of cultural hybridity.

Nativist thinking and the privileging of Northern European culture was supported by the work of criminologists such as Lombroso, who claimed that crime was largely the result of biology. The criminal was inferior in the sense that he or she had inherited traits or characteristics that drove him or her to engage in unlawful behavior. Such a view corresponded with the nativist strategy to limit immigration, incarcerate criminals, and sterilize persons arrested and convicted of breaking the law. This climate of fear and suspicion of foreigners and things foreign and the belief that one's genes were responsible for one's behavior, a school of thought known as biological determinism, found their way into the discourse about Mexican American youth gangs.

In the 1920s, Emory Bogardus (1926) began collecting data about the problems encountered by young boys then living in Los Angeles. Relying primarily on interviews with teachers, community leaders, and newspapers stories, Bogardus concluded that the problems experienced by young boys in Los Angeles at that time called for a proactive stance on the part of the entire community. Like the progressives, Bogardus never questioned the beliefs, values, and attitudes cultivated by Western civilization. In fact, for Bogardus, Western civilization is *the* answer to the difficulties encountered by teenage boys in Los Angeles in the 1920s. Although he does point out that an economic system should place the interests of boys before profits (p. 108), he fails to present a blueprint for such a policy. He does, however, present a detailed approach for correcting the problems of boys in Los Angeles. Bogardus supports the bureaucratization of the study of delinquency—physicians, psychologists, social workers, and the police all working together to find "solutions" to the "problems" encountered by boys in urban centers. Although he includes some statements from Anglo boys who were interviewed as part of his research, his is a "top-down" approach to the problem of juvenile delinquency. That is, professionals study a problem and propose solutions, which are then imposed on those who are said to need help. The assumption is that professionals know best. This attitude is evident in his description of "disorganized" and "gang" areas of the city. Bogardus refers to maps—an approach known as the Cartographic School of Juvenile Delinquency (see Sutherland & Cressey, 1978, cited in Shoemaker, 1984, p. 70, and Shaw and McKay, 1969)—that "show distinctly where social disorganization is going on" (Bogardus, 1926, p. 144). He goes on to interpret the activities occurring in parts of the inner city as a call for action.

> The challenge offered by the districts which are producing centers of petty and grand larcenies, sex delinquencies, "gang" destruction of property, and the creation of vicious attitudes on the part of the boys, is perfectly clear. (p. 142)

Bogardus never doubts in the bureaucratic approach to the boy gang problem. That it might contribute to the multiplication of the gang phenomenon is a question he never raises. His model is strictly unidirectional. Professionals and experts direct solutions to those areas where boys with problems are found. Bogardus writes that it is the duty of the juvenile correction system to set the boy who has gone astray back on the right track.

> It is their (correctional agencies) main business to follow back along the crooked trail to the origins of trouble, to straighten out distorted reactions, and to set the boy going along constructive paths. (p. 127)

In this statement, one can find the basic tenets of an approach to juvenile delinquency known as control theory. The elements that define control theory are the search for the cause or causes of the delinquency, the altering of behavior and/or beliefs, and the placement of the boy in a more constructive environment, the "constructive paths," as a means for controlling future behavior. It is, however, Bogardus's endorsement of the quintessential symbol of social control, eugenics, that firmly ties him to the control theory of delinquency.

> The eugenics movement needs encouragement to the extent that every boy may be "well-born" with sound physical equipment. Training for marriage and parenthood is a minimum which will build a race of "well-born" children. (p. 140)

Through this quotation, Bogardus's connection to the work of Lombroso and the belief that ultimately science can engineer a law-abiding population is obvious. It should be made clear that the eugenics movement, although popular in the 1920s and 1930s, did not receive unanimous support. For example, Thrasher (1942, p. 404), who conducted studies of boy gangs in Chicago, questioned this approach. While the Eugenics Committee of the United States promoted the idea that gang membership consisted mostly of boys who were genetically defective, Thrasher noted that gang boys he studied in Chicago "gave the impression of normal, and often superior, intelligence and a normal development of emotional responses and sentiments" (p. 405).

Thrasher's (1942) work, the title of which claims to be a study of 1,313 boy gangs in Chicago, includes some references to Mexican boy gangs. Although, as in Bogardus's (1926) work, these are rare, the small number of references to the Mexican boy gang is not surprising considering the number of Mexicans in Chicago in the 1920s in comparison to the number of immigrants from Eastern and Southern Europe. These references by Thrasher to Mexican boy gangs, however, should not be ignored. They are evidence that the Mexican boy gang, while recognized, was not considered as serious a problem in Chicago in the 1920s as boy gangs made up of children of Southern and Eastern European parentage.

Perhaps Thrasher's (1942) most famous contribution to social disorganization theory and boy gangs is the term "interstitial areas," which he defined as the most significant concept of his work (p. 22). By "interstitial areas" of the city, he meant those parts of the urban landscape that represent a break with the older and more established neighborhoods.

> In nature foreign matter tends to collect and cake in every crack, crevice, and cranny—interstices. There are also fissures and breaks in the structure of social organizations. The gang may be regarded as an interstitial element in the framework of society, and gangland as an interstitial region in the layout of the city. (p. 22)

For Thrasher, the social disorganization found in the interstitial areas leads to lifestyles that make the boy gang possible while it makes intervention by social institutions almost impossible. The boy gang and poor neighborhoods are, according to Thrasher, inseparable. In the index to his book, there are four references to Mexicans and Mexican boy gangs (p. 596). One of these is a quotation from one Roy Dickerson about Mexican boy gangs in El Paso.

> In the Mexican section of El Paso is a group of three or four hundred Mexican boys composed of from twenty to twenty-five gangs, each with its separate leader. These gangs have been growing steadily for eight or nine years and now embrace a rather seasoned and experienced leadership in all sorts of crime. (note dated September 26, 1924, in Thrasher, 1942; pp. 380–381)

This portrait of the Mexican boy gangs in the early 1900s is striking in its similarity to the Mexican American youth gangs of the 1980s and 1990s. First, the gang is seen as a growing problem within a geographical space, "the Mexican section." Second, it is perceived as being well-organized and hierarchical. And finally it is involved in crime. Dickerson's note is important for another reason as well. Unless it can be demonstrated that newspapers in El Paso in the early 1920s were printing articles that sensationalized the Mexican boy gang problem, Dickerson's note casts a shadow of doubt over the argument that the news media fabricated the Mexican American youth gang. Instead, Dickerson's note illustrates how the mass media, in conjunction with changing political, economic, and cultural values at the turn of the century, riefied the Anglo's long history of apprehensions and fears about the Mexican American community into twentieth century stereotypes about Mexican American youth gangs.

Review of significant events from the 1820s to the 1920s demonstrates that the demonization of the Mexican American youth gang is not an entirely new phenomenon. The ideas of Mexicans as "foreign," as prone not just to violence but brutal violence, as members of "bandit gangs" have a long and complex history. One significant change in the early 1900s is the association of the Mexican American community with illicit drugs. Understanding the grafting of this "social problem" onto the Mexican American community is also rooted in historical material.

MARIJUANA LAWS

Although the Marijuana Tax Act was passed in 1937, the roots of this federal legislation go back to the early 1900s. Morgan (1990) notes that this piece of legislation was the result of the growth of the Mexican population in the Southwest and not the dangers posed by the drug itself (p. 233). She goes on to explain that, typically, laws that result from "drug wars" reflect political, economic, and cultural fears and pressures more than they reflect threats from the drugs themselves. For this reason, drug legislation is usually a form of social control more than it is a method for dealing with a threat from some chemical substance (p. 233).

The association in the public mind of marijuana with the Mexican American community originated in the early 1900s (Bonnie & Whitebread, 1974, p. 30; Himmelstein, 1983, p. 22). It was not until the late 1920s and early 1930s, however, that marijuana became a drug perceived as a social evil that must be controlled. Before the 1920s, the use of marijuana was seen as confined to Mexican immigrants. The build up of the marijuana drug war in the 1920s coincided with an anti-Mexican campaign. The dramatic increase in Mexican immigration in the early 1900s led members of the Progressive movement to argue for immigration reform. Their fear of foreign customs and values was manifested in complaints about the growing Mexican population. Mexicans were said to pose unfair labor competition, drain social service budgets, and monopolize some small-business enterprises. Professional and civic organizations and labor unions also joined the crusade to curb immigration. Their primary fear was that Mexicans would not be able to measure up to middle class expectations for citizenship. Nativists were concerned about protecting "American stock." Urban dwellers were afraid that Mexican laborers might want to move from rural areas into the cities (Morgan, 1990).

The first study of marijuana was conducted in 1914 in Texas along the Mexican border. However, the study found that there was little concern over the use of marijuana and many people were ignorant about the drug (Morgan, 1990). In California, the first marijuana law was passed in 1915 in what appears to have been a need for professional reform and secondarily a reaction to the East Indian immigrant population, which used "ganja."

Henry J. Finger, the man who spearheaded the drive to outlaw the use of marijuana, was a member of the American Pharmaceutical Association (APA) and the American Public Health Association (APHA). The United States was participating in an international medical drug conference and Finger was sent to represent the United States and the APA. His purpose at the conference was international drug control. By 1930, sixteen states had passed legislation against the use of marijuana (Becker, 1963, p. 135).

In 1926, the California legislature reported a connection between marijuana use and the Mexican population (Morgan, 1990, p. 244), but the hysteria about marijuana and the Mexican population would not make its appearance until the mid 1930s, when the head of the Federal Bureau of Narcotics, Harry J. Anslinger, began a campaign that would culminate in the Marijuana Tax Act of 1937.

Using the resources of his organization, Anslinger designed and executed a media campaign aimed at creating awareness about marijuana and bringing the drug under the control of the Federal Bureau of Narcotics. Under Anslinger's supervision, articles about the dangers of marijuana, "the devil's weed," and its close association with the Mexican population, were prepared for newspapers and magazines (Bureau of Narcotics, 1933, p. 61, cited in Becker, 1963, p. 140). Morgan (1990) states that the Mexican population "was the group most closely associated with the use of the drug in the Southwest, so this group easily became the scapegoat" (p. 247). Mexicans were not seen as victims of marijuana use but as carriers of a disease that could infect "America's youth" (Himmelstein, 1983, p. 67).

The demonization of marijauna, its close association with the Mexican population, and a growing population of young Mexican Americans merged with older fears and anxieties dating back to the early 1800s about Mexicans as mongrel barbarians to create a social environment in which the singling out of young Mexican Americans for harassment, humiliation, and physical violence were encouraged. All that was lacking was an incident that the authorities could hold up as "proof" to support the community's fears and anxieties about Mexican Americans and drugs.

SLEEPY LAGOON CASE

The zoot-suit style of dress, popular in the 1930s and 1940s, consisted of baggy pants, long-tailed coats, wide-brimmed hats, and high boots. Ducktail haircuts and ankle-length watch chains were also part of the style (McLemore & Romo, 1985, p. 19; also see Mazón, 1984 for a detailed study of the zoot-suit riots). The significance of the zoot-suit riots is that their sustained coverage by the mass media brought national attention to the Mexican American teenagers of Los Angeles and other parts of the Southwest. The sensationalized reporting about dramatic increases in Mexican juvenile crimes in Los Angeles were later found to be grossly inaccurate (Domer, 1955).

In the 1930s, the focus on Mexican youth gangs in Los Angeles began to intensify, culminating with the Sleepy Lagoon case and zoot-suit riots in Los Angeles in the summer of 1943. The trial of seventeen Mexican American young men for the murder of José Díaz and the zoot-suit riots crystallized the public image of Mexican American youth gangs, which were labeled as *pachuco* gangs in the mass media. While the term "*pachuco*" has an obscure past, it is generally understood to denote someone of low economic and social status (Mazón, 1984, pp. 4–5). After ten years of coverage of "Mexican criminals," increasingly referred to as "*pachuco* gangs" and "zoot-suit hoodlums" by the *Los Angeles Times* during those ten years, U.S. servicemen began an assault on Mexican American adolescents and young adults, only about half of whom were actually wearing zoot suits (McWilliams, 1990).

Just prior to the zoot-suit riots, biological explanations for the behavior of Mexican boys deemed criminal by the police and courts were promoted. The most dramatic example of this perspective was the testimony by Lieutenant Edward Duran Ayres, of the L.A. Sheriff's Department, before the grand jury investigating the Sleepy Lagoon Case.

In August 1942, José Díaz was found dead near a swimming hole referred to as "Sleepy Lagoon." According to McWilliams (1990), Díaz's death lead to the detention of more than 600 Mexican American "gang members." Eventually, seventeen Mexican American youths were convicted of killing Díaz and sent to prison. By October 1944 all charges against the defendants were dropped and they were ordered released (Mazón, 1984, p. 24). Lt. Ayres, testifying to the grand jury investigating the Sleepy Lagoon case, argued that the basis for the Mexican American youth gang problem was genetic. He explained in his testimony that the "Mexican Indian is mostly Indian—and that is the element that migrated to the United States in large numbers" (Mazón, 1984, p. 22). Ayres pointed to the Aztec practice of human sacrifice as proof of the Mexican's disregard for human life "which has always been universal throughout the Americas among the Indian population" (Mazón, 1984, p. 22). Such biologically deterministic explanations for the Mexican American youth gang contributed to an atmosphere that encouraged attacks of Mexican American youths by U.S. military personnel.

Between June 3 and June 13, 1943, U.S. servicemen indiscriminately attacked Mexican Americans in Los Angeles, often while the police looked the other way (Mazón, 1984, p. 76). Many factors contributed to this outbreak of violence: war hysteria, economic depression, frustration due to rationing, as well as anti-Mexican sentiments. The significance of the zoot-suit riots is that their sustained coverage by the mass media brought national attention to the Mexican American teenagers of Los Angeles and those in other parts of the Southwest.

Ayres's explanations for the behavior of Mexican American youth gangs drew on discourses about biological determinism and criminal behavior. Such discourses were not new. Recall that in the 1800s, many Anglos found the idea of mixing of the races to be an abomination. Many of those who wrote about the Southwest pointed to miscegenation, the mixing of Spanish and Indian, as the primary reason for the backwardness of the Mexican people. Recall also that Bogardus supported the eugenics movement as one of several solutions to the problem of delinquency. Indeed, in the 1920s, eugenics was seen by many as offering a promise of improving the citizenry.

In the mid-1940s, the progressive idea of social disorganization in the Mexican American community was expanded by George I. Sánchez (1943) to include the Anglo community. The Mexican boy gang problem was said by Sánchez to be a manifestation of a socially segregated society that legally imposed a system of discrimination. The *pachuco* in Los Angeles, and other cities in the Southwest, was interpreted by Sánchez as a reflection of an unjust social and economic system. Sánchez concluded that:

> The pachuco is a symbol not of the guilt of an oppressed "Mexican" minority but of a cancerous growth within the majority group which is gnawing at the vitals of democracy and the American way of life. (Sánchez, 1943, p. 20)

This proposal by Sánchez is important because it represents the first documented example in which a leader in the Mexican American community questions the assumption of both control theory and social disorganization theory that mainstream culture was an ideal to which minority communities should aspire. Sánchez makes it clear that members of the dominant culture can engage in unfair and unjust behaviors that can lead to negative social phenomena such as *pachuco* gangs. Sánchez points to the contradictions in how democracy was being practiced in the 1940s and views these contradictions as contributing to the creation of Mexican American youth gangs.

Important as this expansion of the "social disorganization" label from the *barrio* to the larger society is in the etiology of the Mexican American youth gang's definition, it is not without problems. First, the model proposed by Sánchez is essentially a passive one. Closely related to this passivity is the linearity of the model. There is little in Sánchez's essay to indicate that the Mexican American teenagers and young adults in the early 1940s were, in some ways, more proactive in their adaptation of the zoot-suit style and other fashions of the time. For Sánchez, discriminatory policies elicit certain behaviors, in this case gang behaviors, in Mexican American teenagers. The *pachuco* lifestyle is presented by Sánchez as a kind of reflex action to an unfair social system. The *pachucos*, as well as the Mexican American community itself, are seen as having something done to them and without the wherewithal to influence the social process. Sánchez's thesis is that discrimination leads to the adoption of the *pachuco* attitude and zoot-suit lifestyle. There is evidence to show that human behavior is more complicated and much richer than such a linear model of cultural production posits. In fact, Mazón (1984) has noted how a history of discrimination, youthful exuberance, and a buoyant wartime economy, among a host of other factors, contributed to the adaptation of the zoot suit by some Mexican American young men in the 1940s. The *pachucos* of the 1940s were anything but passive. McWilliams (1990) cites several occasions when Mexican American teens and young adults took issue with their public image by writing letters to the editors of newspapers in Los Angeles in the 1940s (p. 231). The point is that the *pachuco* phenomenon cannot be accepted as simply a reaction to oppression from the dominant social group. It must also be seen as a form of resistance (see Hebdige, 1979, esp. Chap. 7).

For Sánchez (1943) the possibility and responsibility for changing this oppressive social situation rests with the dominant group. Yet

Sánchez does not explain how the vast majority of Mexican American teenagers who did not adapt a zoot-suit style, described as "squares" (see Moore, 1978), or those who either joined or had serious intentions of joining the armed forces (see McWilliams, 1990), had managed to overcome the barriers imposed by the discriminatory policies and practices to which he refers.

The Mexican American youth gang has been subjected to numerous programs designed to control and in some cases eradicate it. Those writing in the 1940s who advocated assimilation as a solution to the Mexican American youth gang problem could refer to a lack of adaptation to the American mainstream as the reason for the youth gang problems in the Mexican American community of Los Angeles and elsewhere. That is, reasons for the attacks by sailors on Mexican American youths during the zoot-suit riots were localized in the Mexican American teens themselves and their Mexican culture. Humphrey (1945) wrote:

> The recent "zoot-suit riots" in Los Angeles called public attention to the existence of problems of cultural adjustment among the descendants of Mexican immigrants in the American southwest. (p. 69)

Humphrey blames the Mexican American teenagers, about half of whom were not even dressed in zoot suits (see McWilliams, 1990), who were attacked by U.S. servicemen for bringing these attacks on themselves through their failure to adjust to the cultural mainstream.

What the works of Bogardus (1926) and Thrasher (1942), including the note by Dickerson, make clear is that the Mexican boy gang, along with gangs of boys of other ethnic groups, was recognized as "troublesome" at least a generation before the zoot-suit riots of 1942. The works of Bogardus and Thrasher also indicate that while the Mexican boy gang was recognized, it was not considered any more serious a problem, and judging from the quotations in Bogardus's book probably less of a problem, than the boy gangs made up of descendants of Southern and Eastern European immigrants. To argue that the mass media created the Mexican American youth gang is to ignore the acknowledgment by researchers of the Mexican American youth gang as an urban problem long before the mass media devoted undue attention to this subculture within the Mexican American community.

Even the association of youth gangs with illicit behaviors seems to have predated the media's preoccupation with the Mexican American youth gang. Bogardus (1926), quoting a boys' worker, notes that "Boys are sometimes used by druggists to peddle narcotics, and while doing so they learn the use of dope, steal automobiles, and get into sex difficulties" (p. 109). This image, according to the model proposed by Hartman and Husband (1974), could be grafted on to the image of the Mexican American youth gang. Such an association facilitated the acceptance of the drug-addicted Mexican American youth gang stereotype.

What these examples illustrate is that the model of teenage gang behavior, that is, fighting, drug use, theft, and sexual promiscuity, was set by the 1920s. What occurred in the 1930s and early 1940s was a shift that highlighted the role of Mexican American youths within this model to make it appear as if gangs were synonymous with Mexican youth. Bogardus (1943, p. 56) asserted that Mexican boys were serving as scapegoats for the juvenile delinquency problem that did exist in Los Angeles in the 1940s. Holton (1942, cited in Domer, 1955, p. 46) found that the same number of Mexican American boys appeared in juvenile court in the first six months of 1941 as appeared in the first six months of 1942. He concluded that "there is no wave of lawlessness among Mexican children," and he went on to say that, while there was a problem with gang violence, it was being addressed.

Rather than argue that the mass media created the Mexican American youth gang, it would be more appropriate to say that, in the 1930s, the mass media of Los Angeles contextualized Mexican American teens within the model of gang culture that had been defined by popular culture and social scientists using control and social disorganization theories of youth crime. This contextualization included stereotypical views of Mexicans as prone to violent, criminal behavior.

In the 1940s and 1950s, Mexican American youth gangs were the target of government programs aimed a curbing or eliminating gangs. In the aftermath of the zoot-suit riots, government funding to deal with the gang problem was made available. Moore (1978) mentions that in Los Angeles, "these omnipresent programs are part of the normal institutional environment of the barrios themselves" (p. 42).

Barker (1974, c. 1950) published a booklet in which he contextualized *pachuco* slang within historical and economic contexts. Taking a sociolinguistic perspective, Barker provided a history for many of the words used by *pachucos* in Tucson and related their use to the self-esteem and sense of identity it gave the speakers. While far from being an unbiased approach to the terms and phrases used by *pachucos* in Tucson, Barker's work is important because it moved away from an emphasis on the need to assimilate and more toward an emphasis on the need to accept the language of the *pachuco* on its own terms within a social and cultural context.

The 1950s was also the time when the Boggs Amendment (1951) and the 1956 Narcotic Drug Control Act were tacked on to the Marijuana Tax Act of 1937. The Boggs Amendment and the Narcotic Drug Control Act minimized judicial discretion in sentencing for drug possession or sale. These laws also increased the penalties for possession and sale of narcotics (Bullington, 1977, p. 22).

The decade of the 1950s also witnessed the heaviest migration of Mexican Americans, or Chicanos, from rural areas in California to the cities. The major impetus for this migration was the Bracero program, which brought in cheap labor from Mexico with whom Chicano workers could not compete. At the same time, better paying and more stable factory and manufacturing jobs were being made available in the cities (Bullington, 1977, p. 32).

In the early 1960s, psychoanalytic approaches to the Mexican American youth gang became popular. Paz (1961, pp. 9–28) compared the *pachucos* of East Los Angeles with the Mexican national character in an attempt to find solutions to feelings of inferiority, which he claimed were keeping the Mexican nation from attaining its full potential. His esoteric essay, first published in 1961, is a series of observations grounded in the psychoanalytic humanism that can be traced back to Samuel Ramos and José Vasconcelos in Mexico and Sigmund Freud in Europe. There is little concrete data in Paz's essay to support the lofty conclusions.

Heller (1966) also took a psychoanalytic approach to the study of Mexican American youth. While she did not conduct research specifically on gangs (Moore, 1978, p. 43), Heller categorizes Mexican American teenage males into two categories: the "ambitious" boys and the "delinquent" boys. Heller argued that there were specific cultural patterns in the Mexican American experience that pushed young boys into gang, or deliquent, behavior. For her, the real deviants among Mexican American young males are those boys who do not join gangs (Moore, 1978, p. 43).

By the early 1970s, Klein (1971) was taking the opposite view. Categorizing gangs as "traditional" or "spontaneous," Klein argued that the Mexican American traditional youth gang was no different from any other youth gang that could be found in poor neighborhoods.

Ethnicity was not a major factor in distinguishing the Mexican American youth gang.

It was in the late 1960s that a younger generation of Mexican Americans began to appropriate the Mexican American youth gang image as part of their protest against the treatment the Mexican American community was receiving from mainstream institutions, including the mass media. Young Mexican Americans across the Southwest got caught up in *Movimiento* activities. César Chávez's marches in 1966 on behalf of farmworkers received national attention. In New Mexico, Reies López Tijerina organized some members of the Mexican American community and reclaimed land grant rights. In 1968, Los Angeles high school students organized "blowouts" to protest the lack of access to college-track courses. The year before, the Brown Berets and the college organization UMAS (United Mexican American Students), later MEChA (Movimiento Estudiantil Chicano de Aztlan), were organized. At the Denver Conference held in 1969:

> speakers proposed that henceforth most crimes committed by Mexican Americans were to be interpreted as "revolutionary acts." The language and dress of the street youth, the *vatos locos*, would be emulated. *Carnalismo* (the brotherhood code of the Mexican American youth gangs) would mold the lives of the students and become a central concept in the proposed nationalist ideology. (Muñoz, 1989, p. 76)

As they had done with the word "Chicano" itself, which had acquired derogatory connotations, a younger generation of Mexican Americans would embrace the style of the *vatos locos*, which literally translates into the "crazy guys." Instead of "criminal acts," the behaviors would be called "revolutionary acts"; rather than troublemakers or criminals, gang members were transformed into revolutionaries.

By the late 1970s, some community leaders were still critical about the ulterior motives of the police antigang units in tracking Mexican American youths. Some believed that the citing and tracking of Mexican American youth for progressively more serious violations, beginning with truancy, were nothing more than attempts to build a case against young Mexican Americans in order to facilitate their incarceration in state and federal prisons at a future date (Martinez, 1978, p. 9). That is, Mexican Americans picked up for minor offenses or on circumstantial evidence could have their previous arrest record introduced in court to help convince the jury that the individual on trial was more than likely guilty. Such voices would soon be drowned in a rising tide of economic, political, and cultural changes that called for harsher treatment and sentences for "gang members."

The ushering in of the Reagan era in 1980, along with news media reports of the rise in crack-cocaine use, would intensify the negative attitudes of the country's political and community leaders toward gangs and youths of color, including Mexican Americans. The 1980s would see a "darkening" of the population, the aging of baby boomers, and a widening of the income gap. These three factors would do more to contribute to the hysteria about gangs and gang-related crimes than actual crime. The increase in the population of people of color coincided with an increase in gated-community living. Fear of people of color, especially young people of color, led to the search for lifestyles that minimized interaction among affluent whites and impoverished young adults and adolescents. Aging boomers began to direct criticism to the younger generation. Rather than make funds available to assist young people, older whites voted for politicians and propositions that cut state funding for social programs and instead encouraged their privatization. Such votes further isolated young people and almost guaranteed the continued widening of the income gap.

CONCLUSION

This brief history of the news coverage of the Mexican gangs in the 1800s, and later the Mexican American youth gangs, indicates that such coverage has relied on stereotypical themes. For example, the idea of duality, that is Mexicans appearing to be "well-bred dons" but actually leading bandit gangs, makes its appearance in local television news when it becomes impossible to distinguish gang members from the rest of the population of poor, Mexican American young people. For this reason all Mexican American youths are said to be candidates for anti-gang programs and treatments.

The supposed growth of the gang, as the Dickerson note (cited in Thrasher, 1942, pp. 380–381) stated, that these groups of youths are increasing in numbers and becoming well-organized is another recurring stereotype. The Mexican American youth gang situation is reported as a growing problem. Like a plague, the gang problem continues to infect young Mexican Americans.

The income gap of the 1980s created an especially heavy burden for inner-city minority youths. Lack of educational resources and access to jobs that offer a living wage, both due in large part to the movement of businesses from the downtown area to suburban business parks, was a manifestation of dramatic shifts in capital. In this changing environment it became easy to fall back on stereotypical notions and beliefs about Mexican American youths and to reinvent many of the myths about the Mexican American youth gang that have worked so well in the past. It is in this context that the resurgence of the news media's (especially local television news) coverage of the Mexican American youth gang is examined next.

Chapter 3
Influence of Newsworkers

> When I broke into reporting in the early '50s on the *Los Angeles Mirror*, minority murders were called "misdemeanor homicides" and went uncovered—unless a Mexican American teenager killed another Mexican American teenager. Then it was a "gang war" and made page one.
> —C. Ericksen, 1981, p. 7

> The time when [reporting on gangs in this town] was really bad it was over-hyped by the media. It was something that wasn't there.
> —Mexican American female TV reporter, personal communication

The first chapter of this book provides an overview of newswork, with an emphasis on the production of the Mexican American youth gang story, as a social process. It shows that newsworkers do not go about their business of reporting in social isolation. Rather, they work in a professional, social, and cultural setting to which they are intimately connected in a myriad of ways (Gans, 1980; Kaniss, 1991; Schudson, 1995; Tuchman, 1978). One way that they are connected to these settings is through the history of the profession. Reporters are as much a product of history as is the Mexican American gang story itself (see Chapter 2). Chapter 2 outlined how both the profession of journalism and the reporting of Mexican crime are the products of economic, technological, and political conditions. As a result of this historical process, certain parameters have developed about what is or is not considered "news." Television news reporters must learn what these parameters are and adhere to them or risk being marginalized or even dismissed from work (Breed, 1955; Serrin, 2000, p. 9; Sigal, 1973).

Reporters are also a product of the journalistic training they receive in schools and on the job. Students learn how to "do broadcast journalism" in journalism classes and in television newsrooms. Lessons about what makes a good story, how to write or produce a good story, and what attracts viewers' attention teach a television journalist what and what not to produce as "news" (Shoemaker & Reese, 1991).

Equally as important as the training they receive are the routines of news production to which reporters adapt. These routines tie the journalist to the professional, social, and cultural systems that impose certain limits on what broadcast journalists do. Journalists have to work within a system of news production that is bigger than any one reporter or station for that matter. The Mexican American youth gang news story may at times originate in the newsroom, but it would not get the airplay it does if did not get support from other persons and organizations outside the newsroom.

In the following pages, newswork and ties to the culture in which television news reporters produce news are examined. The Mexican American gang stories journalists produce for local television news are intertwined with the cultural setting, which in turn is intertwined with the prevailing attitudes, ideas, and values of the social, political, and economic system. In this chapter, I will focus on how the training journalists receive, both formal and informal, cultural setting in which they work, and the practices that make up their work all contribute to the structure and content of the Mexican American youth gang story for local television news.

WHY STUDY ROLE OF NEWSWORKERS?

It is important that we understand the role of the newsworker in the production of the Mexican American youth gang story because such understanding can provide a basis for productive strategies designed to minimize and eventually eliminate the stereotypical representations of Mexican American youths currently seen on local television news. If, as gatekeeper theory argues (White, 1949), it is found that newsworkers, especially assignments editors, producers, and news directors, have a great influence over the form and content of the news stories they produce, then education at an individual level would go far in helping to minimize the negative representations of Mexican American youths on local television news. Such a finding would also support the argument to diversify newsrooms, since newsrooms staffed with individuals from different backgrounds and with a broad range of experiences would result in a wider range of news stories and perspectives.

If, on the other hand, newsworkers are responding to directions from corporate managers and cues from government leaders, as political economy theory argues, or the wishes of the audience, as liberal-pluralist theory proposes, then more complex approaches are required to fight the stereotypical notions found in news stories about Mexican American youth gangs. If this last case turns out to be more accurate of news production than the first—the gatekeeper theory—then educating newsworkers while ignoring the structural features of newswork or the role of audience demands in the production of news will not likely result in less stereotyping of Mexican American youths. A more sophisticated approach to the education of newsworkers would be required. Such an approach would examine the role of the newsworker within the larger news culture to find the subtle ways that individual reporters might influence the newsmaking process as well as how structural features of newswork influence newsworkers. This of course does not mean that diversifying newsrooms should not be a priority. It does point to the need to recognize that diversity alone may not automatically lead to better news coverage. This is the play of influences we want to be alert to and begin to identify in the examination of the production of the Mexican American youth gang news story.

PRODUCING GANG NEWS STORIES

In 1993, a reporter with one of the local television news stations produced a three-part series on gangs titled *Ganging Up*. In this series, as in most that deal with Mexican American youths, there should be evidence of how the history of news coverage, the training reporters receive, and the routines that they carry out in the process of making news influence their work. The series is examined here as an example of these influences.

The *Ganging Up* series was heavily promoted by the station. It consisted of three, two-and-a-half-minute segments that ran on consecutive nights as part of the 10:00 P.M. newscast. Each segment started with the reporter live from a section of the city in which gangs were said to be a serious problem. Following the reporter's brief introduction, a preproduced segment on some aspect of the gang problem in the city was aired. After the segment aired, the reporter would once again be seen on air for concluding remarks and, at least for segments 1 and 2, promotion of the next two segments.

In the first part of the series (segment 1), viewers were given an overview of the extent of the gang problem in the city. For much of this footage the reporter and a news photographer had ridden with the police and videotaped young people out late at night. During one of the evenings when they were out riding with the police, a fight between two individuals was caught on camera by the photographer. In the second part of the series, viewers saw young men in a detention center and a boot camp program for gang members. The third segment was on a boxing program for juveniles at the Pan American Recreation Center. The transcript of segment one follows:

Ganging Up, March 1993

Video	Audio
Anchor sitting at desk with over-the-shoulder graphic "Ganging Up."	All too often you hear of young Austin teenagers, many of them gang members, committing crimes left and right and paying only a small price for their actions. But some say the gang problem here in Austin has eased. But as channel [X]'s reporter tells us in Part 1 of her series, Ganging Up, others insist that gangs in Austin are simply changing.
A potpourri of shots in slow motion and blurred, hazy: A person on a stretcher being placed in an ambulance; a Mexican American youth in handcuffs being taken away by police; close-up of an officer's arm as he picks up a gun obviously found at the scene of a crime; police car at crime scene; African American teens "throwing signs" then hamming it	*Reporter's voice:* Several months ago a teenager in Austin is gunned down and killed by San Antonio gang members. We heard rumors of retaliation by local gangs but as of yet no major violence. It seems gangs in Austin and troubled teens are focusing on other things these days, but they are still hanging out till all hours of the night.

up for the camera. They end by singing "Gotta have a piece of that Kit Kat Bar."	
Mexican American teenager is walking away from the camera, alone.	*Reporter's voice*: They are doing and selling drugs.
Night. Officer, Street Crimes Unit. He is demonstrating for the camera how drugs are sold at a particular corner.	The way they do it is this guy will see, he'll be looking, and he'll look and these guys are selling. He'll say "rolling" and that means the police are rolling up. So these guys will hide the dope.
Police stopping car with African American teens.	*Reporter's voice*: They're committing crimes . . .
Police aiming flashlight inside the car. Faces of teens appear blurred in the video.	*Police officer*: OK, are you aware this is a real heavy dope dealing area? And you guys are under age and you have no driver's license.
Officer's voice (Street Crimes Unit) over nighttime shots of graffiti; officer shining his flashlight on wall and "reading" graffiti.	Once they're drunk they'll go out and do, spray graffiti all over the place. And then they'll go steal a car. I've never seen this guy's tag. He's new here. And this guy here, he's, I think he might be in the penitentiary.
	Reporter's voice: And they're willing to do it again and again.
Night. Exterior. African American teens.	*Voice-over of police officer*: We used to run into a lot of kids who got like six things, arrests, and they're still out here running around on the street.
More exterior night shots of teenagers.	*Voice-over of police officer*: Oh, I've seen them go to the Garner House

	for doing a shooting and mamma comes to get them and an hour later they're out. And then they're back out on the street laughing and their friends say "well so-and-so shot somebody and nothing happened to him" and so now you see these kids carry guns.
Slow motion of African American teen pointing to his temples, obviously playing up to the camera.	Experts say gangs are much savier [*sic*] now and have turned their attention to selling drugs, stealing cars, anything to make money, although violence is still a factor.
Mexican American youth on a sidewalk or street, victim of shooting or stabbing. Mexican American teen in handcuffs. Mexican American teenager on stretcher, paramedics getting him ready for transport to a hospital.	*Voice of police officer*: Kids these days don't have respect for anything. They don't have respect for themselves. They don't have respect for other people. They don't have respect for their property or your property. And most of all they don't have respect for your life. I mean it's nothing for them to get a gun and just kill you.
Exterior. Reporter screen right. Police car with flashing lights in the distance, screen left.	Right now I'm at the corner of 12th and Chicon where a lot of teenagers hang out till all hours of the night. There are a lot of bars and clubs in this area that are attractive. But take a look at some of the most recent police statistics for the metropolitan area. In 1992 there were close to 700 gang-related offenses, that's up 3.6% over 1991. Of those offenses there were almost 700 arrests of gang members and their associates. That's up 28.5% from '91. So there are more arrests being made these days but as you'll see from this series quite often juveniles don't stay behind bars very long, if at all.
On-screen graphics.	
Back to the reporter.	

Anchor in newsroom conversing with reporter.	How many of those arrested last year were under 18?
	More than half of them were under 17 and many of them committed the most major crimes such as murder, assault, robbery, and burglary. Tomorrow night we're going to be talking about the Juvenile Justice System, what works, what doesn't work, and what's being done to change it.
Anchor	Disturbing report. Thank you.

In the introduction to this story, the anchor, a white male, tells the viewers about "hearing all too often about teenagers, many of whom are gang members, committing crimes and getting away with it." However, he fails to mention that it is newsworkers who report such stories to the audience. Research has shown that most people learn about crime and other illegal activities in the community through the news media. The news media disseminate such information to the public. The anchor's introductory remarks create the impression that the news and information broadcast to the public is unrelated to the newsworkers and system of news production that distributes such information. By ignoring the connection between "hearing all too often" and newswork, the remarks promote the idea that the information provided to the viewer is "objective" and "true." The fact that topics for news stories are selected and developed, that is, molded or produced to fit the television news format, is a process that remains invisible. Many researchers, such as Males (1999), contend that the news media habitually exaggerate youth crime, and this introduction to segment one of the series, in fact the entire *Ganging Up* series, would qualify as an example of such an exaggeration.

In the introduction to segment one, information about teenagers and gang members taking advantage of the criminal system is presented. The implication is that the laws that deal with teenagers and gang members today are outdated. The introductory remarks indicate that the teens and gang members of today are different from those of the past. Since the teenagers of today are different from those of yesterday, new ways of dealing with these lawless teenagers and gang members are in order. A common theme in my research with newsworkers, indeed with many adults, was the idea that teenagers today are qualitatively different from the days "when you and I were growing up." One newsworker said that when she was in school, the biggest problem she and her friends got into trouble for was chewing gum in class. Today, she went on, kids are carrying guns to school (personal communication).

This discourse, about teenagers being "different," that is, more violent and willing to break the law, was captured by the term "superpredator," which was introduced by Bennett, DiIulio, and Walters in their book *Body Count* (1996). In it these authors reported that "a new generation of street criminals is upon us—the youngest, biggest, and baddest generation any society has ever known" (1996, p. 26). The year before the publication of *Body Count*, Wilson (1995) had written how U.S. citizens "are terrified by the prospect of innocent people being gunned down at random, without warning and almost without motive, by youngsters who afterwards show us a blank, unremorseful face of a seemingly feral, presocial being" (p. 492). Such terms—superpredator, feral, presocial—conjured up images of young people as subhuman. The idea behind such terms was that because the United States had experienced a high number of births in the late 1970s and early 1980s, especially in communities of color, the country could expect a dramatic increase in crime in the next ten years, when those poor, inner-city children entered their teen years. The myth of the superpredator predicted the taking over of society by African American and Latino urban youths who would have no moral compass, would be hyperviolent, and would have total disregard for any middle-class values or beliefs. Bennett, DiIulio, and Walters (1996) presented Bureau of the Census data projecting a dramatic increase in the growth of black and Latino youths. While the white juvenile population was expected to grow by 8 percent between 1990 and 2010, the black juvenile population was expected to increase by 26 percent and the Latino juvenile population by 71 percent (p. 26). There is little doubt that in the public mind the term "superpredator" is strongly associated with black males (Mauer, 1999, p. 126). However, the public's fear of crime is not limited to the association of crime with African Americans. Crime is also associated with other minority groups, including Mexican Americans in the southwestern United States.

Another point raised in the introduction to the series is that the decline in gang activity is an illusion. Rather than an actual decrease, what is in fact happening, according to this introduction, is that gangs are changing. The sources for this information about the changing nature of gangs are simply identified as "some" people and "others." This type of reporting reinforces the stereotype of gang members as able to disguise themselves and hide activities from law enforcement agencies. It is reminiscent of the *Dons* in dime novels about the old West who could lead double lives, one as respectable cattlemen and another as leaders of bandit gangs (Pettit, 1980).

Thus, in the introduction to the first segment on gangs, the tone for the entire series is set. Before one electronic frame of the series, or "package," produced by the reporter has aired, a contextual frame for what viewers will see on their television screens has been created. That frame consists of "teenagers, many of whom are gang members, committing crimes left and right." That frame is a television news frame and not a reflection of crime statistics, which remained stable through the early 1990s and then began to show a decrease. In fact, the same station that produced the *Ganging Up* series reported in December of that same year that Austin was one of the safest cities in the country. The same anchor who introduced the gang series reported later in the year that "Despite what seems like increasing violence all around us, Austin is actually showing a decrease in the number of violent crimes this year. . . . Of sixty-three large cities Austin is considered one of the safest. . . . It is sixtieth on the list. The question remains, if crime is down, why are folks here so afraid?" That local television news was fueling people's fear of crime, that is, cultivating a fear of crime, was, of course, never brought up (Gerbner et al., 1994, pp. 17–41).

In addition to reports about a decrease in crime, FBI statistics indicated that many more adults than teenagers were committing crimes. Most of those teenagers who were getting into trouble, including Mexican American teenagers, had never joined and would likely never join a gang. Indeed, most teenagers would never even get into trouble with the law. The words and images in the *Ganging Up* "package" that follow the introduction serve to reinforce, not challenge, the anchor's comments and the news frame they created.

An important point to keep in mind is how in the introduction to the *Ganging Up* series the anchor has managed to equate "teenager" with "gangs." In his introduction, as well as in the mind of his audience, there is little difference between the two. The word "gang" implies inner-city minority youth (*Newswatch*, 1994, pp. 28–29). Equally significant is that ethnicity is never mentioned. There is no need. Instead, the camera will focus almost exclusively on African American and Latino males as symbols of the gangs currently threatening the city. It is members of these two ethnic groups, but primarily Mexican American youths, who are featured on camera as examples of gang members who are "doing and selling drugs," "committing crimes," and "willing to do it again and again."

When the series opens, the reporter is seen standing in an area of town that has a significantly high ethnic population. The public's perception of this geographic space as prone to criminal activity, an area where gangs, drugs, and violence are common, is reinforced by the newscast. To further tie the area to an image of crime and mayhem, police statistics are introduced by the reporter. The image of "objectivity," of "fair" reporting is supported by official data from the police. Such numbers help promote the belief that what is being reported is not only accurate but true, when in fact the collection of official statistics has been criticized for promoting the official views of a society (Kitsuse & Cicourel, 1963; Males, 1999, pp. 25, 26, 32). For example, official crime statistics have been shown to be quite flexible depending on the political climate. Wright (1985), citing a study by the Police Foundation, notes that local arrest statistics can be misleading. He goes on to write that "the data are often manipulated for political reasons" (p. 32).

The gang script analyzed above is an example of how official views about Mexican American youth gangs, including statistics, come to be incorporated into local television news. By studying the process of production, we can come to appreciate how these official views are seamlessly woven into the discourse of Mexican American youth gangs.

DECIDING TO MAKE NEWS

When asked how she decided to produce a story on gangs, the reporter who put the three-part series together replied that it was her idea. She had attended a press conference organized by a state representative to announce the findings of a statewide committee assigned the task of studying the problem of juvenile crime in Texas. A pamphlet distributed at the press conference recommended changing state laws to better deal with the problem of youth gangs. At the press conference, the representative pointed to weak and outdated laws that did not allow authorities to deal effectively with the juveniles of the 1990s, who were responsible for increased crime rates. The reporter thought at that time that the problem of juvenile crime and especially gangs would make a good series.

The next step was for her to talk to the assistant news director, who agreed with her that the topic would make a good series. Together they decided that the series would cover the extent of the problem of gangs in the city, profile success stories, and show the community how to change the situation of gangs, in other words, offer solutions for the problem of gangs. The two of them worked out the logistics of producing such a series.

After the logistics had been approved the reporter began making phone calls to her sources. She contacted members of the Street Crimes Unit and made arrangements to ride with the unit at night. She called administrators of the boot camp for juvenile offenders and also contacted administrators at the Juvenile Detention Center, which is known for holding "at risk" juveniles.

> Once you get approval you're pretty much on your own, I'm pretty much on my own, to set my own schedule. I start making calls. I sit down and make zillions of calls, connections, people. I decide kind of how I want to do it, whether I want to do two parts, three parts, what angles I want to cover, you know, like if I want to cover the police angle I make a lot of calls to, ah, different divisions within the police department. If I want to cover the juvenile justice angle I call the courts, I call the attorney, the juvenile justice detention center. I also call several organizations who provide a lot of assistance to gang members and ask them for success stories. (TV news reporter, personal communication)

Thus, the strategy for collecting the information that will be shaped into a three-part series on gangs begins with the police and moves on to the court system and then on to community organizations. At no point did the reporter mention making an effort to interview a gang member or members. The closest she got was former gang members, and these she contacted through either the police or community agencies. Again, this pattern of collecting information predisposes the content of the story to favor a criminal justice view of the gang situation. It is that view that will get the most play on a series.

The reporter explained that in the first part of her segment, she wanted to show viewers "what it was like to be out on the street."

She said that she asked the police she would be riding with to take her and the videographer to places where she would be able to capture this life on the streets: "I just asked the police officers to take us where there's a lot of criminal gang activity on a regular basis." They were driven around in the eastern part of the city and for the "live" intro to the first segment the broadcast originated from a street corner in this part of town, an area with a significant Mexican American population. When I asked why she went with the police, her response was that the parts of town where she was taken were areas she would not go without a police escort. According to her, these are high-crime areas where not only she and the videographer would be in danger but the station's video equipment might be damaged or stolen. For these reasons she explained that she would not travel by herself to these high-crime areas of the city. In contrast to her perceptions, another reporter at the same station, who is Mexican American and female, said that fear of going into the part of town that has the highest concentration of poor and working-class Mexican Americans is a problem among many of the white reporters at the station. She also said that unlike many white reporters, she had no fear of walking alone in that part of town and often does. She also added that she had no fear of walking up to Mexican Americans in that part of town and starting conversations with them (Mexican American reporter, personal communication, February 20, 1994).

The series on gangs proved to be successful in some measure. For example, the reporter who produced the series told me that the police were interested in obtaining a copy of the series to use in presentations to community organizations, parent groups, and others to tell about the problem of gangs in the city. Also, everyone at the television station thought it was a good series.

The steps taken by the reporter to produce this series are almost a textbook case of "good journalism." The reporter picked up on a theme that was of great concern to a prominent leader in the community, a state legislator, and to many in the community as well, a prime consideration when producing news, but especially local television news, which depends more on attracting large numbers of viewers rather than specific demographics (Kaniss, 1991, p. 103). The three-part gang series localized a problem that was receiving national attention at the time. The reporter discussed the idea with, and got the support of, her supervisor, the assistant news director. Next, she contacted her sources in the community who, because of her past reporting, knew her. Finally, with the photographer, she produced a three-part series for inclusion in the local newscast.

The dependence on police sources for information about gangs raises questions about how fair or objective a series like *Ganging Up* can be. Rather than a comprehensive view of the "gang" situation, the report delivers the criminal justice interpretation of the gang problem. The police, juvenile justice administrators, and district attorneys all provide a criminal justice view of gangs. In the second segment of the three-part series, even the interviews with persons in boot camp, who are held in detention, cannot be said to be free of the criminal justice view. After all, how free is someone to express his or her views on their confinement while being held by the state? In addition to this type of organizational pressure on the production process, it must be remembered that the directors of the institutions, not the reporter, select who will appear on camera.

> I went through the captain out there [the boot camp] and said, here's what we need. We need to talk to some former gang members who are in there because of gang-related crime. We want to talk to them about how this program is changing them, what they think about it. I said can you help us. He said "well we'll single out some people for you to talk to and we'll have a group. We'll talk to them all beforehand." (TV news reporter, personal communication)

During our interview, the reporter went on to explain why not just anyone would do for an on-camera interview. One of the purposes of the profiles, or sound bites, is to support information presented in the program. These news stories need individuals who will not criticize but, instead, acknowledge the benefits of the boot camp.

> We told them [boot camp administrators] we want someone who speaks well, someone who will come across well on camera. Someone who is not going to sit there, say it's a gang member who's only been in the program for fifteen days, he's probably still going to have a bad attitude and if we're sitting there asking him, you know, why are you in here, what has this program done for you? He's going to sit there and go, you know, FU, basically. You know? I mean, or he's going to sit there and say "yes," "no," you know? You need someone who is going to verbalize his feelings and talk about what his life was like in a gang, and what the [boot camp] is doing [for him], that sort of thing. (TV news reporter, personal communication)

The selection of persons to speak on camera is controlled by the supervisors of the correction facilities. It is also influenced by the needs of the newsworker, which were established to a great extent by how she decided to approach the story. The story structure called for success cases that could be used to show others that help is available and that leaving the gang lifestyle behind is possible. Ignoring how sources for information are selected and how decisions about on-camera representatives are made hides the subjectivity involved in producing stories such as this series. Another way to mask the subjective nature of such stories is through the presentation of numbers.

The official statistics on gang-related offenses are presented to the viewer as a kind of "proof" of what the rest of the news story is arguing. However, in the absence of an agreed upon definition of the term "gang," what good are numbers that purport to be a measure of "gang-related" activity? Under such circumstances, statistics can be used to support almost any argument. It makes little difference that reporters cite the police as sources for their statistics on gang-related offenses. Beyond the problems that are largely due to a lack of agreement on the definition of terms, there are distortions in gang stories that are due to the way numbers are selected by reporters. Some police officers who provide statistics about gangs to the news media claim that newsworkers, not the police, distort information about gangs.

Police officers contend that all information about gangs in the city is made available to the news media. Reporters then take that information and by prominently featuring some numbers and ignoring or downplaying others, for example, that many gangs reported in police statistics no longer exist, can create the impression that the gang problem is worse than it actually is.

When asked about this, reporters replied by saying that they simply report the statistics provided by the police. Reporters interviewed for this study seemed unaware that the police were giving them numbers that included gangs that no longer existed. Most of the reporters interviewed for this study were asked, "Where do you get the statistics about gangs that appear in your stories?" Each one replied "the police." No reporter said that he or she had ever questioned the police about their information on gangs. The use of police statistics showing a growing problem with gangs and crime, like the statistics in the *Ganging Up* series, becomes even more difficult to explain when the same station later that year reported FBI statistics indicating a drop in crime (see p. 69).

In his introduction to Part 3 of the series *Ganging Up*, the anchor stated that "Here in our city, experts say there are about 25 active gangs and as many as 100 gang-like splinter groups." Viewers are never told whose definition of a "gang" is being used and what that definition is. Does the definition include gangs that are "nonexistent" or have evolved into other gangs? If so, why?

In addition to getting an inadequate definition of the word "gang," reporters also fail to ask the police what exactly is an "active gang"? How does it differ from an "inactive gang"? What is meant by the phrase "gang-like splinter group"? Such terms and phrases, and their unquestioned acceptance by newsworkers, indicate that stereotypical notions based on common sense are creating the story of Mexican American youth gangs more than hard data or evidence about Mexican American teenagers and "gangs."

Another reporter, working for a competing station, also produced a three-part series on a program designed to give gang members self-confidence and improve their self-esteem. The reporter, who covered the crime beat, went on his daily rounds looking for news at the police station, the courts, and other agencies associated with the criminal justice system. When not able to go to the police station, he would call to ask if anything newsworthy had happened. He also frequently checked in at municipal court. This reporter, like many others interviewed for this study, admitted that he was dependent on his sources, by which he meant persons and official records and institutions that gather information about crime in the city (Mexican American TV reporter, personal communication).

This reporter first heard about the PURGE (Prevention of Urban and Rural Gang Evolvement) program from a probation officer working at the Juvenile Justice Department. The reporter said that the probation officer told him that he could be trusted because, in the past, he had given the Juvenile Justice Department fair representation on the air. For this reason, the probation officer allowed the reporter to shadow him for three months. During this time the reporter was learning about the program and planning his production. Soon the reporter was interviewing parents on camera and videotaping teens as they took on the challenge of an obstacle course in the woods.

According to this Mexican American reporter, who was the newest crime beat reporter in the market, getting access to information had not been easy. When he was first assigned to the police beat, he was out of the loop. This "outsider" status had a direct impact on his reporting:

I didn't know how the system worked. I didn't know what the hierarchy was and who was chief and who was lieutenant, who was sergeant, who was patrol officer. So I had to learn from scratch. It took me several months, I mean I was getting my butt beat on different stories because, you know, it would be a little story that everybody was interested in that those [other] reporters would have but I wouldn't have simply because they knew people. They knew how to go down there, they knew how to talk to people, they knew who to call, people would call them with ideas because people knew them on the beat. I didn't have that luxury because no one knew me. (TV news reporter, personal communication)

In these examples of gang series produced by local television news, by no means unique in both production and content, can be seen evidence of how the relationship between reporters and their sources influences the collection of information that is used to produce the gang series. These two reporters produced material for local television news by staying within their circle of sources. It is almost unthinkable that they would go outside that circle to gather material for stories. This is partly due to the circumstances under which they work as well as their training as journalists. Writing about the beat system and its relationship to the coverage of resource-poor groups, Goldenberg (1975) notes that newspaper reporters tend to think more and more like the people and organizations they cover. Furthermore, beat reporters begin to write for the officials they work with and not for the consumers of news. Goldenberg goes on to explain that, after a while, beat reporters and their sources "became a close-knit club in which only the members really understood what was happening and only the members would truly appreciate a good story" (p. 79). This process of tying the reporter to his or her sources and the organizations they represent and how this influences the production of the Mexican American youth gang story is examined next.

NEWSWORKERS AND NEWSWORK

The relationship of newsworkers to the process of news production has been addressed by several researchers (Allan, 1999; Altheide, 1976; Gans, 1980; Gieber & Johnson, 1961; Herman & Chomsky, 1988; Shoemaker & Reese, 1991; White, 1950). Some researchers have concluded that newsworkers have little or no influence on the selection and production of news (Altschull, 1995; Gans, 1980; Herman & Chomsky, 1988). This group of researchers, usually arguing from a political-economy perspective, tends to argue that economic priorities and organizational structures and the routines of news production impose too many limitations on newsworkers to allow for any opportunity to present material that does not conform to professional expectations and organizational guidelines. In general, their view is that the owners of capital who have invested in news media and through the years have set up the system of collecting and distributing information have tremendous influence over what gets produced as news. Their findings lead to the conclusion that it is absurd to expect the owners of media to allow the dissemination of news and information that might threaten the economic system or the social system that has contributed to the wealth and influence of the news media that they own.

What these authors fail to explain, however, is how news organizations can at times present reports that directly challenge the authority of the state or a private corporation. For example, in late 1999 and early 2000, the *Los Angeles Times* reported on the Ramparts scandal within the L.A. Police Department. The report stated that officers in the antigang, antidrug Ramparts Division of the LAPD violated the law by harassing and intimidating people, mostly Latinos, planting evidence used to incarcerate innocent victims and, in one case, shooting one person without provocation (McDermott, 2000). Such exposure of the corrupt and illegal practices of some L.A. police officers on the pages of the *Los Angeles Times* is difficult to explain within the political-economy model.

At the other end of the spectrum are those theorists who propose a liberal-pluralist perspective of news production. These theorists argue that newsworkers have tremendous leeway in not only what is presented as news but how it is presented as well. Rather than a conspiracy among the elite to keep material it perceives as a threat off the nation's television screens, computer screens, magazines, and newspapers, this group of investigators argues that reporters are responding to the audience's needs for news and information and to the owners' need to sell commercial time or newspapers. According to the liberal pluralists, the free market, made up of various interest groups that includes millions of consumers, rather than a small elite community, is responsible for the news that is produced (Allan, 1999, pp. 49–50). The strength of the liberal-pluralist perspective is that it recognizes that consumers do have some influence over what gets produced as news. The dependence of the news media on advertising that, in turn, depends on consumers who are attracted to news stories is a real factor in profit-driven journalism. However, the liberal-pluralist perspective fails to explain why the media can be used to inflame a community's fears about youth crime when no real threat is posed (Males, 1999; Mazón, 1984). Logically, persons in the community would, by virtue of their everyday experiences, be able to discern that no real gang threat as presented on local television news exists.

These two opposing theoretical perspectives, the political economy and the liberal pluralist, each contribute a partial explanation for the production of the Mexican American youth gang news story. What they both lack is an ethnic perspective on the matter of youth gang hysteria. While the production of news in general may be explained to some extent by these two theoretical perspectives, both fail to recognize and explain the role of ethnicity in the production of these stories.

While reporters proclaim that they report the facts in an objective manner without consideration of an individual or community's ethnic makeup, studies have shown that there are significant differences in how ethnic groups are presented by the news media (Entman, 1992; *Newswatch*, 1994; Vargas, 2000). One difference appears to be the willingness to portray members of ethnic groups, such as Latinos, Asians, and African Americans, as members of gangs while resisting such portrayals when covering white youths even when those white youths are involved in similar criminal behaviors (*Newswatch*, 1994; Williams, 2000, p. 108). Explaining such differences within a cultural model of news production requires a perspective that includes ethnicity as a factor in the process of news production.

Although newsworkers are fond of promoting themselves and the work that they do as "objective," "balanced," and "value free," Gans (1980), Schudson (1978), and others have pointed out that no one, not even newsworkers, operates in an environment that is absent of values and cultural beliefs. We are all born at a certain time and in a certain place. In the process of growing up, we learn certain values and beliefs that contextualize our experiences. Those values and cultural beliefs, what sociologists refer to as "social glue," serve to hold a community together (Durkheim, 1965). The stories a community tells, including news stories, can only make sense within a certain cultural context that has integrated certain values and beliefs into the social fabric, including values and beliefs associated with different ethnic groups. It is in this sense that we can speak of Mexican American gang news stories as "intertextual" phenomena. That is, Mexican American gang stories are related to other aspects of culture without which such stories would not make sense. It is almost impossible not to notice that gang stories are overwhelmingly about African American or Mexican American youths. Despite evidence that most of the young people in this age group will never join a gang or be in trouble with the law, stereotypical thinking about criminal activity in these groups of young males makes such news stories believable to the audience. The strength of these beliefs is tied more to white, middle-class fears and perceptions than to hard data (Males, 1999, pp. 8–10).

In the previous chapter, the history of the coverage of Mexican American youth gangs was discussed. An understanding of that history helps us understand why we get the kinds of stories about Mexican American youth gangs that we see on local television news today. That history also helps us understand how reporters, as part of the culture, come to accept certain assumptions, ideas, and opinions about Mexican American gangs without question. Such assumptions, ideas, and opinions make their way into stories about Mexican American youth gangs. Those assumptions are the basis for much of the distorted reporting about Mexican American youth gangs.

For example, news stories, including the example presented earlier in this chapter, often report that Mexican American gang membership is increasing. However, some researchers, for example Morales (1982, p. 141), report that gang membership is relatively stable over time. Other news stories promote the belief that there is something unique about persons designated as gang members. However, many researchers report that they are impressed by how "normal" many so-called gang members appear and behave. Another popular assumption is that Mexican American gang membership is generational, that is, membership in a gang is said to continue because a gang member's father and grandfather were in the gang. These myths persist despite evidence to the contrary (see Moore, 1991). Many police officers said that the primary reason that Mexican Americans join gangs is that the father, older brothers, uncles, or some other family member had been in a gang. In the course of my research, I never came across a Mexican American teenager or young adult who told me that his father or grandfather had been in a gang, yet this type of thinking is deeply ingrained in some people in the community. A white female crime reporter explained to me during our interview that, in the Mexican American community, being a member of a gang was often a family tradition. She added quite nonchalantly, "You were probably in a gang when you were growing up." No Mexican American reporters, videographers, or administrative staff I spoke to while conducting research ever suggested that I had ever been a member of a gang. The female crime reporter's assumptions about Mexican Americans were the basis for her conclusion that, since I am Mexican American, I had probably been a member of a gang as a teenager.

Another misconception is that Mexican American gang members are sociopaths willing to rape and kill for no apparent reason. In fact, according to studies by Zatz (1987) and Moore (1978), most persons identified as gang members are not involved in violent criminal behavior. Nor are Mexican American gangs involved in highly organized criminal activities. Most of the groups referred to as a gang in local television news stories are nothing more than a loose association of friends and acquaintances. Even police officers assigned to work with gangs admit that Mexican American youth gangs are not highly organized (Romo & Falbo, 1996, pp. 84–85).

This is not to say that there are no young, violent criminals among Mexican American young people. Certainly there are some Mexican American teenagers and young adults who act out and hurt and even kill others, but this type of behavior is hardly unique to Mexican American youth. What is not unique is the willingness of reporters, especially white reporters, to ascribe this type of behavior or the potential for this type of behavior to the population of Mexican American young people even when there is data indicating just the opposite.

A key assumption underlying the reporting about Mexican American youth gangs is the objectivity of news. The myth of objectivity in newswork makes it difficult to engage in discussions about biases and racism. To understand why it is that newsworkers cling to the idea of objectivity and how it can influence the reporting on Mexican American gangs, it is necessary to examine the history of this professional ideal. Other features about news reporting that contribute to distorted stories about Mexican American young people are related to the economic system within which news is produced, the socialization of reporters, and how newswork is organized.

OBJECTIVITY IN NEWS

Objectivity in the news is a relatively recent development (Schudson, 1978). Prior to the "penny press" of the 1830s and the professionalization of journalism in the late 1800s and early 1900s, readers did not expect the material they read in newspapers to be free of bias or presented in a fair and balanced manner. Just the opposite: Readers expected the news they read to promote a point of view, opinion, or philosophy. The point of view, opinion, or philosophy being expressed in a newspaper was typically that of the owner of the paper. The owner might be an individual or an organization, including a political party. Those were the days of what has come to be known as the partisan press. The partisan press was in large part supported by subscriptions from readers. Some ads may also have appeared in the partisan press, but these did not account for a significant amount of revenue. Those who did not agree with the opinions or philosophy in the paper could voice their protest by writing to the editor—who felt no obligation to publish the letter—or simply cancel their subscription or, more likely, simply quit buying issues of the paper.

The ushering-in of the era of the "penny press" in the 1830s changed the economic basis of news production. Readers no longer paid for the cost of producing the news they read. Instead, advertisers began paying for the attention of readers. The cost of newspapers declined because advertisers began to subsidize the gathering and processing of news in return for access to potential customers. News was no longer being sold to subscribers; rather, news became a means for attracting readers who were in turn being sold to advertisers. Thus, the relationship between newsworkers and their readers, later with the introduction of radio and television news, their listeners, and viewers, was altered as a result of economic changes that were being reflected in both the form and content of newspapers.

On the one hand, this change contributed to the democratization of news. That is, when news went from a subscriber base, which meant small audiences and higher prices for newspapers, to an advertiser base, which meant larger audiences and lower prices for newspapers sold to the public, newsworkers were forced to pay more attention to the material that would attract readers. More people than ever before were having an impact on what would be defined as news. On the other hand, more does not necessarily mean better or improved. The middle-class consumers that advertisers were trying to reach with ads in newspapers did not develop free of prejudices and fears. Selling newspapers to this literate and growing middle class meant incorporating its values and beliefs into the news, including fear of "others," such as Mexican Americans in general and Mexican Americans believed to be members of criminal gangs in particular. Thus, what is called "objective reporting" is still very much rooted in the prevailing ideas and practices of the time.

In a free-market system, the economic motives that underlie news production are one reason for questioning the concept of objectivity in the news (see Gandy, 1982; McManus, 1994, p. 42). This is because the economic system organizes how people act and live. The organization of behavior can have a tremendous, but not absolute, influence on how people think. That is, what an employee is willing to do to collect a wage can have a strong influence on what system of thinking is developed to justify such behavior. In this context, beliefs about what newsworkers do, that is, reporting the news objectively, can be seen as both influences and products of economics and the organization of newswork and not some core ideal separate and apart from daily routines.

The professional ideal of "objectivity" in the news then is a cultural belief. Value-free reporting can be said to be one of the highest held values of newsworkers. It is within this professional and economic context that a reporter working on a story about Mexican American youth gangs carries out his or her journalistic activities. Before any information comes into the newsroom about a possible story about Mexican American youth gangs, the newsworker is already confined by a professional belief in objectivity and a pledge to value-free reporting. These beliefs and values are reinforced by a series of professional activities designed to attract an audience, maximize profits, and produce stories in a timely, cost-effective manner.

Economic factors, then, must be considered when examining the influences on the Mexican American youth gang story. This is because in the United States, local television news is a for-profit activity within a market-driven economic system. In the larger television markets, investors in television stations typically expect a return of from 25% to 50% on their investment, depending on the competition and the demographics of the market. Reporters are acutely aware of these pressures, although initially most will deny that they are in any way influenced by them. While we might give reporters the benefit of a doubt and accept that reporters are not *directly* influenced by their station's need to show a profit, it would be naive to argue that some pressures are not influencing newsworkers in some way. The hiring of consultants by television stations in order to "improve" the newscast is one way that newsworkers are reminded that they are in a competitive business. Newsworkers submit videotapes of their stories to consultants who are usually hired by the television station's parent organization. These consultants examine a newsworker's stories, including the video, writing, and on-air presentation. Periodically the consulting agency sends reviews to the newsworkers to help them "improve" their presentations. All reporters are aware that the purpose of these critiques is to increase audience share for the purpose of increasing station profits.

One reporter who had been in the business for ten years pointed out that the big difference in television news reporting in the early 1980s, when she first started as a television journalist, and the early 1990s was the increased pressure to produce stories. Because of the availability of new UHF and cable channels, there was also increased competition from other channels, which meant that newsworkers had to work harder to attract viewers. In addition to increased competition from new television stations and cable channels, the downsizing of television news departments, the larger number of journalism majors seeking employment, and the diffusion of high quality, portable, and easy to operate video equipment all contributed to heavier workloads for newsworkers. The diffusion of sophisticated yet easily operable video equipment led to the availability of video stories from satellite services like Conus Communications. Such services lessen the dependence of the local television station on its newsworkers, since the station can acquire stories via satellite from anywhere in the country or the world. These changes were motivated more by the need to remain competitive and thus increase profits than improving news coverage.

However, the increase in profits is to a large extent dependent on maintaining and expanding the television audience. Rather than invent new formulas and introduce new styles, the producers of local television news fell back on the themes that had worked for popular media in the past: violence and sex, what some critics of television news have called "irrelevant coverage" (Diamond, 1975, p. xiv).

Local television news has a long history of focusing on sex and violence in order to attract an audience. Stories about disasters, such as car accidents and fires, and about personal tragedies, such as murders, rapes, and other forms of violence are the types of stories that have made local television news something of a joke (Kaniss, 1991, p. 101).

The Mexican American gang story serves this tradition of focusing on sex and violence well. The themes of senseless violence, such as drive-by shootings, gang fights, and initiation rituals during which members are forced to "walk the line," and loose morals, exemplified by the sexual activity of gang members, and illegal activity, such as selling illicit drugs and acquiring and distributing stolen guns, made coverage of the Mexican American gang by local television news hard to pass up. The economic and organizational pressures discussed earlier encourage TV journalists to fall back on stereotypical stories. Under pressure to produce stories faster and attract and hold an audience, a reporter could not ask for better raw material than the stereotypical Mexican American youth gang. Such stories practically produce themselves.

As members of the community, newsworkers share many more beliefs and values with their viewers than they disagree about. As newsworkers, they have been initiated, so to speak, in the techniques of news production within the culture of news, which is part of the larger culture, with all its biases and prejudices. Thus, even before a news story on Mexican American youth gangs is produced, a context of values and beliefs is already in place that will influence the content and structure of such stories. The social and educational backgrounds shared by reporters reinforce their values and beliefs.

PROFESSIONAL VALUES

Many reporters today are trained in university departments of journalism. These departments are closely tied to both the profession and business of journalism. Often it is retired or working newsworkers who teach in the local college or university department of journalism. By teaching a younger generation of reporters how to produce news, older reporters, either intentionally or unintentionally, pass on their system and style of reporting. Moreover, textbooks used in journalism classes are often written by working or retired journalists. In addition, schools of journalism often invite newsworkers to present lectures and workshops on journalism practice. This "closed" system of initiating newsworkers into the field allows for the profession to recreate itself with every new generation of newsworkers. In this way ideas about what constitutes news and how best to collect information that can be used to produce news are passed on from one generation of journalists to another.

In the three newsrooms where I spent time observing the newsmaking process, all except one of the reporters I interviewed said that they had graduated from college. The one who had not graduated had dropped out of a journalism program in order to take a job as a television news reporter. Most of those who had graduated had received degrees in journalism. Others had degrees in history, English, communication, or some other field in either the humanities or the social sciences. Thus, virtually all of the reporters interviewed were college educated. Some, such as news directors or anchors, had, or were working toward, master's degrees in journalism.

In addition to the tendency to recreate itself, the system of initiating newsworkers into the profession after they have received their degrees is also overwhelmingly managed by whites (Heider, 2000). Whites hold 82% of the television news jobs across the nation (Newkirk, 2000). By sheer numbers alone minority perspectives, including those of Mexican American reporters, will have a hard time garnering support in such an overwhelmingly white profession. The pressure to "write white" has been addressed by several writers (Newkirk, 2000; Santos, 1997). The term refers to the sense many minority reporters have that their editors or producers want them to write stories about minority communities not the way that the minority reporter sees it, but how the white producer would write such stories. The "write white" phenomenon is an indication that simply hiring minority reporters is not a guarantee of "balanced" reporting.

Many Mexican American television news reporters, like other minority reporters, leave the profession because of low wages and lack of opportunities for advancement (Heider, 2000, p. 18). While it is undeniable that minority reporters have been hired with greater frequency in the last three decades, the goal of having fully integrated newsrooms reflecting the communities they cover and report about by the year 2000 has proved to be an elusive one (Quintero, 1998).

University departments of journalism and the practice of journalism are related to the culture in which both evolved and continue to exist. The practice of journalism, and the way it is taught in schools or departments of journalism, is influenced by the culture in which it operates. In turn, culture is influenced by the practice of journalism. In the previous chapter we saw how understanding the coverage of Mexican bandit gangs at the turn of the twentieth century was tied to the racial and ethnic tensions of the time. It would be sheer folly to believe that the reporting on Mexican American youth gangs today is not similarly influenced by racial and ethnic tensions that exist in the general population.

INFLUENCE OF NEWSWORKERS

As reported by Kaniss (1991) and Goldenberg (1975), there is a close working relationship between television newsworkers and the police. One reporter I interviewed spoke of "schmoozing" with police officers. Another spoke of gaining the trust of the police by using information to produce stories that the police find not just "fair" and balanced, but helpful, as the request by the police for the *Ganging Up* video to show during their presentations in the community demonstrates. Here again is an example of how shared beliefs and values help the newsworker, especially the crime beat reporter, negotiate interactions with the police. Reporters and the police are often from similar social and educational backgrounds. However, just because the two professional groups share many social and educational backgrounds should not lead to the conclusion that their relationship is equal. Newsworkers need the police more than the police need newsworkers (Chibnall, 1977). This is because, as discussed earlier, newsworkers are dependent on the police for information that can be processed into news stories. A newsworker who finds himself or herself without material for news stories will soon be out of work. A police department or individual officer that does not make the evening news will continue working. This tilting of the relationship in favor of the police makes television newsworkers aware that if they want to continue receiving information, they must stay on a police department's good side. Their stories about Mexican American youth gangs must include—either explicitly or implicitly—the police department's point of view. While this does not mean that only the police department's point of view may be aired, it does mean that alternative views to those held by the police will have a harder time being presented as legitimate forms of discourse.

There are factors that influence how newsworkers' reports on the Mexican American youth gang will be constructed. One such factor is directly rooted in the beat system. A newsworker might be hired first as a general assignments reporter, but this does not exonerate him or her from the beat system. General assignments reporters will find themselves sent to cover stories that do not fall within the "beats" of other reporters or to cover stories when the beat reporter is unavailable. Because it offers more security and greater prestige, many general assignments reporters attempt to move up to beat reporting. Some, however, are quite happy working as general assignments reporters because they enjoy the variety the position offers. As one reporter said, "I'm a general assignments reporter and that's fine with me because I never know what I'm going to be doing when I walk in the door."

A beat reporter has more of a routine than the general assignments reporter. A beat reporter finds himself or herself coming into contact almost on a daily basis with a small group of persons who can supply information for news stories. This information then is the currency reporters use to get airtime and build their professional credentials both in the newsroom and in the community. The reporter's need for information with which to produce stories and maintain a presence on the screen brings the newsworker back to the "beat" on a daily basis. Such intense contact over an extended period of time ties reporters to the organizational culture about which they report. Such a relationship raises still more questions about the objectivity of the reporting.

Among the various beats a reporter may be assigned to cover is the police beat. Covering the police beat, as all of the police beat reporters I interviewed related, consists of starting each day with a visit to police headquarters, staying in touch with police officers, and keeping tabs on what the city council and other government bodies are doing that might affect the police department.

At the police department's headquarters Public Information Office, the reporter will request the police blotter to see if any newsworthy arrests were made overnight. Some small talk with persons in the Public Information Office will invariably be made. One reporter said, "I schmooze with them because it's good to have them on your side" (reporter, personal communication). From the PI Office, the reporter might then walk down the halls talking to police officers about their work and asking if they know of any leads that might develop into newsworthy events. Such relationships are crucial to the television news reporter's success. Recall the police beat reporter quoted above who related how he was left out of the loop early in his career simply because he was new while his competition at the other two stations in the market got access to information. Such quotes demonstrate how a personal, as opposed to merely a professional, relationship with the sources of news facilitates the flow of information, the raw material, from which news stories are constructed. Newsworkers learn quickly to cultivate these relationships with the police in order to be able to produce stories for their stations.

Another factor that contributes to the successful negotiation of the beat system is the sharing of social values. A long-term personal as well as professional relationship with sources is facilitated when the parties involved share similar opinions, beliefs, values, and outlooks on life. This sharing of values and beliefs facilitates the construction of news stories because much of the information the police department disseminates can be incorporated into news stories unchallenged by reporters. In the absence of television news reporters who have beliefs, values, or opinions different from those held by the police, stories about Mexican American youth gangs easily become conduits for the transmission of the beliefs, values, and opinions that underlie police work.

In the course of their work, newsworkers have opportunities to meet some of the city's most prominent citizens, such as the mayor, city council members, county commissioners, state officials, and even some federal officials. Their educational background, television presence, and access to community leaders gives newsworkers some status in the community. This is a form of what Bourdieu (1986) refers to as cultural capital. The salaries of newsworkers in the market where this study was carried out, while varying greatly and depending on experience and title, tend to fall at or just below the median income. Thus, their educational background, presence on television, and income places television newsworkers squarely within the middle class sector of society.

In addition to their status in the community, television news reporters are often asked to visit elementary and high schools where they discuss their work. In this capacity, they serve as role models for young children in the community. At one television station management encouraged newsworkers to get involved in community organizations. "Our station is a member of the Chamber of Commerce. I learn things that are useful to us and things that we can work with to try to make the community better. I try to stay active and I encourage management and staff to stay active, serve on at least one board or committee because I think we need to give back in that respect as well" (Station manager, personal communication). The rationale for encouraging involvement in the community was that it helps the news team understand what viewers want to see in the newscast.

Not surprisingly, then, as members of the middle class, newsworkers hold many of the values, opinions, and ideas of this social group. On the other hand, most adolescents who live in areas of the city identified as having a gang problem are among the poorest members of the community. Thus, the middle-class status of the newsworker, and consequently the values and beliefs associated with that status which are constantly being reinforced by the work setting, serves as a filter through which information about Mexican American adolescents passes, is evaluated, and is interpreted before it becomes a news story.

In the case of the Mexican American reporter, this middle-class status intersects with ethnicity. Mexican American television news reporters are well aware of their minority status within the newsroom. Several freely admitted that they were hired because the ethnic composition of the community called for a Mexican American reporter on the news team. They are aware that their presence on the news team serves to attract an audience from the Mexican American community. Every day these reporters negotiate an identity that is a mix of their Mexican American identity and their identity as "objective," that is, white, television news reporters. A small number deny that ethnicity is, or should be, a factor in their reporting. They purport to be doing nothing more than practicing their profession as would any other television news reporter regardless of ethnic background. Their goal is to be fair, balanced, and objective regardless of what issue or community they are covering.

Within the community of Mexican American newsworkers, including photojournalists, there are tensions. Many of these reporters freely admit that they are Mexican American and even claim that, because of their ethnicity, they have a responsibility to the Mexican American community. Such responsibility is usually defined as not producing stereotypical stories and as educating white newsworkers about Mexican American culture. One female Mexican American reporter echoed the sentiments of other Mexican American reporters when she said that much of the racism in the newsroom stems more from ignorance about Mexican culture than from hatred or even dislike of Mexican Americans. Stereotypical ideas about Mexicans and Mexican culture, according to this reporter, had to be overcome by educating white reporters about the reality of the Mexican American community. She saw this as part of her role in the newsroom. However, some in the community, after saying that they personally thought this particular reporter was a very nice person, said that the station was not going to allow her to produce any material that went against the stereotypical notions about the Mexican American community.

Other Mexican American reporters, while admitting their ethnic background, deny that this is, or should be, a factor in how they report the news. They see themselves as professionals, the same as any other reporter of whatever ethnic background, carrying out professional duties and responsibilites in an "objective" manner.

Several of the Mexican American reporters I spoke with expressed skepticism about the gang problem. For example, one Mexican American reporter said: "The time when it was really bad [about two or three years ago] it was over-hyped by the media. It was something that wasn't there."

Another Mexican American reporter with a different station, when I asked him about gang stories on the news, looked around, frowned, and moved his arm up and down in a masturbatory, "just jerking off" motion. Finally, another reporter, a Mexican American male, who had produced a series on a neighborhood that was supposedly having major gang problems, answered, in response to a question about whether he would work on other gang stories in the near future: "To tell you the truth, I really don't believe [this city] has that big of a gang problem. I just don't see it."

One white female reporter, while talking about how the police see the gang problem, said that "the cops tend to talk big a little bit. They see conspiracy in everything" (personal communication). Yet, when it came to gangs, she was a firm believer that there was a serious gang problem in the city. She was not unique. All of the white reporters I spoke with expressed regret over the gang situation.

Anchors tended to have a dismal view of the gang situation. One said:

> I recognize that there is a gang problem. I don't feel unsafe. My chances of being a victim of gang violence are slim because of its concentration in the center area of town. I carry mace. It's sad. It's a complex problem. (Female anchor, personal communication)

Her coanchor said:

> When I got here in '87 it was not much of a story. It wasn't that big of a problem as it was perceived by newspeople. I don't know if it relates to getting on late—getting on the bandwagon—we probably were. But I think it mushroomed through the years and there is a lot of publicity now. I wish we could find a magic pill to get rid of the problem. (Male anchor, personal communication)

Thus we see disagreement on the extent of the gang problem among newsworkers. On the one hand there is an ethnic division in the perception of the Mexican American gang problem. Mexican American reporters tend to be more skeptical about the "gang" problem than white reporters. There also seems to be a hierarchical division. Reporters, who are closer to the problem because they leave the newsroom and go out into the field, are more skeptical about the gang problem, while the anchors are more inclined to accept the Mexican American gang problem as defined by themselves—news media, as demonstrated by the words "it mushroomed through the years and there is a lot of publicity now." It is these anchors, not reporters, who have the final say over how a story is written. As one anchor said, "If I have to go on camera and read it I should have the right to edit it" (Male anchor, personal communication). More research about these differences needs to be conducted.

The reporter may also be controlled by the footage that the videojournalist gets in the field. It is considered good television journalism to write to the video that is available (Brooks et al., 1999, p. 451). "Writing to the video" means that the photojournalist can influence the construction of the Mexican American youth gang story through the initial selection of the scenes recorded on video. In one segment on gangs in the city, a reporter explained how she used this technique after finding out that she would not be getting permission to videotape what she had requested:

> Well, they [the administrators of the detention center] apparently misunderstood, or didn't have the approval from higher up for us to get any shots of kids on the grounds. So you'll notice some of the shots we used were just of empty beds, slippers on the floor, that happens a lot too, you'll get things set up and you'll be expecting to get certain things, and then you'll get there and they'll say "Well I'm sorry, we didn't get this approved," and "We didn't understand what you needed, so you can only get this." So that was kind of a downfall for us. But it worked, you know, I wrote to that. (Reporter, personal communication)

The reporter had to rewrite her script to accommodate the video that was shot by the photojournalist. In this way photojournalists can influence a story by selecting certain activities to videotape and not others. However, this influence is limited in the sense that a photojournalist who continuously ignores a reporter's requests for certain video will not be requested by reporters in the future and may even find that reporters will specifically ask the assignments editor not to assign the photojournalist to a particular story. Such a reputation will soon isolate that photojournalist. If he or she does not change, then management will terminate such an employee.

Often police officers or social service workers provide information about gangs that is used to create more methodically produced stories. At two of the stations I studied, reporters had, before my arrival, prepared, far in advance of their air date, three-part series on gangs. Parts of the series featured Mexican American gangs exclusively.

Usually, though, both Mexican American and African American teenagers are included in these reports. One station had produced a three-part series on gangs in March 1993 and a two-part story that aired November 24, 1993, at 6:00 P.M. and 10:00 P.M. Another station aired a three-part series on gangs on May 11, 12, and 13, 1993. Some of these series aired during sweeps periods, yet when asked if the stories were related to "the sweeps"—the ratings periods when television stations attempt to capture the highest number of viewers in order to set advertising rates—the reporters who worked on these stories or series usually answered that it was a coincidence. One Mexican American reporter said that he found it sad that his station would use such themes to boost ratings but quickly added that, on the other hand, these were well-produced series that addressed important problems in the community.

Another equally important finding is that the information gathered from sources is not simply repeated for viewers but instead used to construct narratives about the Mexican American youth gang. I do not use the term "narratives" loosely. Several times reporters told me that they plan and execute their reports within a story format, that is, a report structured with a beginning, middle, and end. In fact, most reporters were proud of the fact that they could tell good stories, even if the material they had to work with was not very exciting. This should not be interpreted as a negation on the part of reporters of relating the facts. Rather, reporting the facts is seen as compatible with telling a good story. None of the newsworkers I interviewed ever questioned how the narrative structure might influence the reporting of the "facts."

At one station there was a poster board on the wall titled "Five Goals of Great Storytelling."

1. Teach the viewers something they don't know.
2. Make it simple and easy to understand.
3. Focus on the people affected.
4. Choose an interesting and/or timely topic.
5. Use compelling pictures and/or sound bites.

It is remarkable that these were not the five goals of great *reporting*. The emphasis here clearly is on "stories."

This preoccupation with telling good stories can lead to distortions in reporting on the Mexican American gang. As with most good stories, it is that which is unique and unusual that provides the best material—what is known in the news business as "man bites dog." Distortions of the Mexican American youth gang can occur through commission as well as omission. One reporter, commenting on the media's coverage of violence in the community, said that while she believed newsworkers were accurate in their coverage, focusing on one aspect of a story can distort the picture the viewer receives of what is actually happening. Focusing on a handful of Mexican American teenagers in an antigang program ignores the overwhelming majority who will never join a gang.

A Police Administrator stated in an interview:

> If you have a shooting that occurs in certain areas of town, the first question asked by the media is, "is this a gang-related incident?" We [the police] don't know. Maybe, maybe not. If we say "maybe," "the police suspect that this may be a gang-related incident" is what you see in the headlines or what you see on the news because it has gotten to be like a buzz word now. It's all gangs. What we find is that a great majority of this is just fights between two individuals. The fact that one or more of them may belong to a gang that we know about doesn't make it a gang-related incident. But by the virtue that just one of them belongs to a gang, it then becomes a gang incident to the media. (Personal communication)

This is obviously a more proactive stance on the part of the news media that is being described here by the police administrator. With respect to stories about youth gangs, the police will rarely, if ever, be seen or heard stating that a person or persons arrested are members of a gang. It is more common for the reporter to state that "police believe those arrested are gang members," or "the suspect is alleged to be a member of a gang." While persons may be referred to as "the suspect" with respect to a certain crime, the police and television news reporters only include allegations and personal beliefs to associated persons with criminal activity when the issue of gangs is raised, and then only when minority teenagers and young adults are involved. Such allegations and beliefs influence the tone and production of the gang story on local television news. The newsworkers can cast a shooting, a fight, or a drug bust in a different frame, the gang frame, than that used to report crime in general. The gang frame taps into the viewers preconceptions, biases, and fears and simultaneously reinforces those preconceptions, biases, and fears.

This review of how television journalists go about their business of producing Mexican American youth gang stories demonstrates how the history of the profession, the training journalists receive, and the routines associated with newswork all influence the production and selection of video and audio that make up these stories. Individual journalists, especially Mexican American journalists, may have ideas about the Mexican American youth gang problem that are different from those held by producers and anchors, but the culture of the newsroom exerts tremendous pressure on journalists not to produce stories based on those ideas. It is important to understand that no one directs these reporters to not produce such stories. Rather history, education, and professional routines keep the journalist from venturing beyond the commonsense thinking found in newsrooms. However, this is not to say that newsworkers have no influence on the production of the Mexican American gang story.

Newsworkers can and do influence the production of the Mexican American youth gang story on local television news. In the course of their work, reporters actively search for and develop ideas for stories. These ideas reflect the mainstream thinking found in the larger community, the police department, and the newsroom. Like their white counterparts, Mexican American reporters seem to be absorbed by the culture of the newsroom and not given much of an opportunity to present alternative views to those found in the mainstream culture, which they are a part of by virtue of their educational background, lifestyle, and profession. By focusing on an issue, such as gangs, and further highlighting only certain aspects of that issue, such as drive-by shootings and drug use, newsworkers can promote an image of the Mexican American gang that does not coincide with the experiences of these youths but with the stereotypical expectations held by newsworkers and television news viewers regarding these youths. Training, social status, newsroom culture, and professional routines constantly pull reporters toward the "commonsense" perspective about youth gangs. Taking an alternative view of the Mexican American youth gang and producing news stories that incorporate such a view would require a major disruption of the newsmaking process.

In the following chapter, I will examine how the police can also influence these stories. The television news reporter is kept closely tied to the police who serve as sources for such stories. By controlling access to information about youth gangs, the police can assist a reporter with his or her work or create hurdles that may become impossible for the reporter to clear.

Chapter 4
Police Influence

> We actually had a meeting with them [the news media] at one point and said "Look, you're killing us on this," I said. "If it's a gang-related incident fine, you have a right, you need to report that. And that's fine. But don't give the name of the gang, because that causes retaliation by either the other group or just another gang that wants their [*sic*] name in the paper, or their name on the news." Now, you'll see gang events up there but you'll never see a name of a gang mentioned.
> —Police Administrator, personal communication

The tendency in studies of Mexican American youth gangs and the news media has been to ascribe great, almost absolute, power to the police. While the police may have tremendous influence on the production of Mexican American youth gang stories, it is important to keep in mind that they are still only one of many organizations competing for attention from the news media. The belief that the police can control the production of news stories about Mexican American youth gangs is an oversimplification that overlooks the influence of other persons, groups, and organizations on the news-making process.

In this chapter, I examine how the police interact with the news media and influence the production of local television news stories about Mexican American youth gangs.

In Chapter 2 we saw how the history of Mexican American and Anglo relations, including economic, political, and social factors in the southwestern United States, influenced, and continues to influence, the production of Mexican American youth gang stories. In Chapter 3 we examined how television news reporters and the process of news production influence the Mexican American youth gang story. The focus of that chapter was on newswork itself. With this chapter, the focus shifts to the influence individuals and organizations outside the newsroom can have on the production of the Mexican American youth gang news story.

In previous chapters, evidence was presented to show how the history of Mexican American and white interactions and the organization of television news today influence the production of Mexican American youth gang stories. Other social forces can also influence the production of Mexican American youth gang stories. In this chapter, I will examine how and under what conditions the police influence the production of these stories. We will see that the police not only compete with other groups and organizations for the opportunity to influence the Mexican American youth gang story but may even at times compete among themselves as well.

GETTING TO THE SOURCE

Interviews with police officers leaves little doubt that the police can and do influence the production of the Mexican American youth gang story. Police officers spoke freely and openly of how they worked with the news media to alter the reporting on gangs. One example clearly indicates that the police can be proactive in terms of reporting on the Mexican American youth gang and, equally as important, that the news media are willing to go along with the police. The quotation below is related to the concern the police had about the effects of identifying gangs by name in the news media. The belief was that naming the gangs in news stories gave them some legitimacy and intensified rivalries among gangs:

> We had an in-service training for all the people in the news media—all the TV channels were there, the newspapers . . . all the anchors were

there and we said "Please help us. We don't mind you selling newspapers or selling your television commercials or whatever, but please don't put the name of the gang in the write-ups in the newspaper or the TV. You know, it's fine to say police think it is gang involvement, gang members are suspected, but don't put Latin Kings or whatever." And after they started following those guidelines that we gave them things got better. (Police officer, Gang Unit, personal communication)

This example demonstrates that the police can get the attention of the news media and ask that they alter their reporting. Another quote about the news media from a police administrator indicates that the request to withhold gang names is not an isolated incident. The police have agreements with the media on other matters, such as hostage situations, about what reporters may say on the air:

We've made a lot of strides with the media. We have an agreement in a number of areas of what will and will not be reported. (Police administrator, personal communication)

These examples show that the police went to the news media to ask that certain information, the names of gangs, for example, be kept out of television news programs and newspaper stories. Officers spoke about agreements with the news media of what they would or would not report. These quotes clearly indicate that the police can influence the production of the Mexican American youth gang story. The police can also influence the Mexican American youth gang story by influencing the gangs themselves.

STRUCTURING THE GANG

The police can influence the production of news stories about Mexican American gangs by encouraging members of different gangs, who may not ordinarily interact, to come together at one time and one place. This is exactly what happened when the police department organized baseball games for gang members. This well-intentioned plan, modeled on a similar program in Los Angeles, California, was designed to provide gang members with constructive and organized activities. Several officers admitted that this plan was a big mistake. The idea behind the police-sponsored baseball games was to channel gang members' anger and competitiveness into sports. The plan backfired. One police administrator explained:

We probably did as much or more damage as the media, in terms of legitimizing the gangs, because we created baseball games for gang members to give them something else to do. Well, the bottom line was most of these gang members, particularly the street level gangs that we have problems with, are poor kids. I mean they come from *poor* neighborhoods, and what we were essentially telling them was, "you can't afford to play little league baseball, we know that. But if you're a gang member the police will form a league for you but you can't get into it unless you're a gang member." (Police Administrator, personal interview)

The result was that some adolescents living in poverty who had never been members of a gang and would never have considered joining a gang were given an incentive to do so or at least to publicly proclaim themselves gang members in order to play baseball. When these "gang members" arrived to play ball, the news media gave them airtime. In response to a question about whether or not the local media covered these games, one police officer stated: "Absolutely. Every time we had one [a baseball game] all the radio, TV, local media, yea, was [*sic*] there, without question."

The quotation above indicates that the police can influence both local television news and Mexican American youths who are stereotyped as gang members or persons said to be in danger of joining gangs. The police have the resources to attract media attention. They can provide sports imagery as part of their strategy to stop gang activity in the community. They also have the resources to attract young Mexican Americans, some as young as ten or eleven, to participate in baseball games on the condition that they admit to being gang members.

The news media coverage of these baseball games among "gang members" raised questions—and fears—in the minds of many citizens about the number of gangs in the city. As a result of the publicity given to these games, the city found itself, almost overnight, with hundreds, perhaps thousands, of "gang members" it previously hadn't known about.

The example of organizing sports events points out how the police can provide the local media with "positive" stories about youth gangs as well as enhance their own public image by providing organized sports activities as an alternative to "gang" activity. The local media, because official sources, in this case the police, were providing the information and organizing the event, obliged by airing stories about the sports events as an "antigang" strategy. However, an unintended effect was that some citizens began to worry about the number of gangs in the city. Still others began to complain that the part of town where the games were being organized was being portrayed as overrun by gangs, which they claimed was not true. Finally, there was a sense among highly placed police officials and state officials that some citizens had begun to question the police department's ability to handle the gang problem.

The end of the organized "gang baseball" events came when the police got word from Los Angeles that these activities were having a backlash effect in that city as well.

> *Police officer*: About the time we realized what happened we were also getting word from L.A., "Hey guys you got to quit this. This is creating a monster."
>
> *Tovares*: Who in L.A.?
>
> *Police officer*: I don't know who it was but L.A. had done the same thing, as had other cities in California, who also had baseball games and they were having meetings. . . .
>
> *Tovares*: Did you have contact with L.A. to develop this program?
>
> *Police officer*: Yea, the officers that were working with the gangs. . . .
>
> *Tovares*: So this wasn't unique to this town?
>
> *Police officer*: (Shaking his head) Everywhere.
>
> *Tovares*: This was [occurring in] other cities across the country?
>
> *Police officer*: Cities across the country were doing the same thing.

The news media did not cover this aspect of the police-organized baseball games. Television news stories explaining to viewers how these games may have contributed to an exaggeration of the number of gangs and gang members were not found in my research of the archives of local television news in the city's History Center. Reports about how poor teenagers living in neighborhoods without adequate resources might be willing to proclaim themselves gang members in exchange for the opportunity to play baseball never appeared on local television news. Instead, as a result of police organized "gang" baseball games, viewers of local television news were left with the impression that the Mexican American youth gang problem was much worse than it actually was.

Another initiative taken by the police may have also led to a false image about Mexican American gang leadership in the area. The police department decided to bring gang leaders together to talk to one another and in this way avoid "gang wars." The problem was that there usually were no designated gang leaders. One officer who had started the gang unit said that Mexican American gangs in that city were not very organized (Gang Unit Officer, personal communication; see also Romo & Falbo, 1996, pp. 84–85). Even much of what was reported by the news media as gang activity was actually the work of individuals and not of a gang. In order to bring gangs together for talks, the police decided to appoint leaders for the different gangs in the area. Inadvertently, the police were giving Mexican American youth gangs a structure. Moreover, in the process of appointing gang leaders and bringing them together, they legitimized this structure. A police administrator explained what happened, and other officers, both in the field and members of the gang unit, corroborated his statements.

> We decided to get the gangs that were fighting [each other] in the same room together. The only way to do that is to find a leader, and so, we— I said we, whoever was running that thing—said, "you're the leader of this group, you're the leader of that group," so again we are going to legitimize you and bring you and sit you down at a table to talk gang-to-gang. *Hill Street Blues* sort of thing. Bring the gangs in and . . . let's get a truce. So when you do that, again it's that whole thing, you legitimize their existence. And that gets publicity. And other gangs that weren't involved in that meeting get mad and they want their names in the paper. So it snowballs. (Police administrator, personal communication)

When these "gangs" came together, the news media reported that the leaders of these gangs were meeting but ignored the fact that the police, not the members of the gangs, had selected the leaders. The news stories that resulted from the coverage of these meetings gave the impression that there were highly organized gangs in the city. In fact, no such gang structure had existed until the police appointed certain individuals as "leaders." Consequently, these "leaders" were often ignored by those who knew them since their leadership role had been assigned by persons from outside the group.

Important also in this example is that the police administrator mentions a television program popular in the 1980s, *Hill Street Blues*, as the model for these meetings. This is important because the entertainment media's influence on the police may have contributed to news reports that exaggerated the gang problem in the city. It is also important because the belief among the police is that the naming of gangs by the news media leads to intensified gang activity. Yet very little is ever mentioned about how a popular television drama might influence the police in how they dealt with youth gangs. The fear the police have about impressionable youth being influenced by television may be in part a projection of their own susceptibility to such influences.

The newsworkers reliance on the police as sources for information about gangs leads to a lack of initiative in the production of stories that may reflect poorly on the police. No stories about these sports events as possibly promoting "gang" activity were ever found in the course of my research at the city's History Center Archives of Local Television News. Nor were stories about police assigning leadership roles to gang members, and the possible consequences of such action, ever produced. Reporters did not produce stories about how the police-organized baseball games had contributed to the illusion that the city was experiencing a growing gang problem.

Instead, local TV news ran only stories that explained how the police were organizing baseball games in order to reach gang members and help steer them into mainstream activities. Even after the police discovered that their efforts were promoting gang identification among the city's poorest Mexican American youths, television news reporters resisted producing stories of how the police department's efforts may have been contributing to the illusion that the town was being overrun by gangs, including Mexican American youth gangs.

GIVING TELEVISION NEWS WHAT IT WANTS

The examples reviewed above indicate that, as persons assigned to control crime and deviance, the police do have some influence on the production of stories about what has become one of the most prevalent symbols of crime and deviance in our society: the Mexican American youth gang. Most researchers who have studied the production of crime news report that the police do indeed have considerable influence on these stories (Allan, 1999; Chibnall, 1977; Ericson, Baranek & Chan, 1989; Fishman, 1980; Hall, et al., 1978; Schlesinger and Tumber, 1994). They generally cite two reasons for this influence. The first is that the police have information collected in the course of their work that can be used to attract an audience. Crime news and stories of deviance, in general, have been supplied to the news media by the police since the days of the penny papers (see Chapter 2). Today stories about crime and deviance continue to "play well" on local television news.

The second reason for believing that the police have tremendous influence in the production of crime news stories is that metropolitan police organizations have departments that make information available to reporters. In addition to providing this information to reporters, police departments are willing to provide the information about crime and deviance in a form that can be readily packaged into news stories. Experienced personnel and the recruitment of persons familiar with the needs of reporters are two ways that the police provide this service.

Most officers interviewed for this research were aware that working with the news media is a long-term commitment that will inevitably include some ups and downs. The emphasis at the police department is on achieving long-term goals. One police administrator said about his experiences with the news media:

> I've been dealing with the media for about eight years now—on a regular basis. So I've learned how to play. [I know] how the game works. If it's a slow news day you can get a decent story on the news and get good video. And you may have the best story in the world, but if it's a busy day you may not even make the 10 o'clock news. (Police Administrator, personal communication)

Having access to persons who know how to work with the news media in order to promote positive stories about an organization is a valuable resource. Such persons can continually interact with the system of news production to learn how best to achieve success over a long period of time. Making information available to the news media on a regular basis, developing a reputation as a reliable source of information, and being available for statements even when the news may not be positive are three strategies that most large organizations, including metropolitan police departments, use to their advantage.

The police department's ability to hire persons with some expertise in media management is another advantage. While local television news has a reputation for poor entry-level pay and short-term contracts, government jobs, including those available to civilians in police departments, offer fair wages, benefits, and long-term stability. It is not surprising, then, that many television news reporters take jobs with government media organizations. Public information office employees often have media backgrounds. When research for this study was conducted, the police department's Public Information Office had just hired two new employees. One of these new employees had a background in news reporting and the other had a background in public relations. The police administrator I spoke with said that part of the police department's plan was to develop long-term strategies for improving the police department's image in the community:

> Hopefully as she [the new hire] gets more comfortable with the police environment, we can start looking at doing some ample packaging to figure out what message we want to get across and how is the best way to get it across.

Having persons with the knowledge about how local television news is produced and what makes a story appealing to the television news reporter can be advantageous to the police department. Such an advantage can give the police a great amount of influence over the production of Mexican American youth gang news stories. In addition, having someone who knows about public relations—the art of creating a positive image of a particular product, organization, or person—also gives the department an advantage over other organizations in the community when it comes to convincing people that the police department's view of Mexican American youth gangs is the accurate one.

In much the same way that education reporters depend on teachers and school administrators for information for news stories and health beat reporters depend on physicians and medical administrators for information, crime reporters, sometimes known as police reporters, depend on the police for information for their news stories.

The connection between a reporter's stories and her sources is considered to be so close that for some it is the sources, not the reporters, that make the news (Sigal, 1973). Such a view, however, is problematic. While sources are important in terms of constructing a story, it must be kept in mind that reporters select their sources. The appearance of sources in news stories is not the result of random selection. Recent complaints from African American and Latino communities to the news media, especially television news, regarding the lack of people of color as sources for stories that have little or nothing to do with ethnic matters are based on the findings that reporters are, consciously or unconsciously, selective in whom they call for an on-air appearance as a source. While sources may make the news, we must keep in mind that reporters also make the news by selecting sources.

In addition to these reasons of why the police can have some influence on the Mexican American youth gang news story, there are other less conspicuous reasons that deserve attention. For example, the police control a variety of resources not available to most other groups or organizations. A steady flow of tax money, trained personnel, and the expectation on the part of the community of professional behavior all give the police department a distinct advantage over other groups and organizations when competing for attention from the news media.

Access to resources is particularly important vis-à-vis the Mexican American youth gang because the latter is made up of a demographic group that lacks access to resources. As one police administrator put it, "most of these gang members, particularly the street level gangs that we have problems with, are poor kids. I mean they come from *poor* neighborhoods." Such an imbalance in access to resources creates an advantage for the police when it comes to communicating with the public via local television news. This imbalance in access to resources is an important point in this context. The police can use the resources at their disposal to promote a view that cannot easily be challenged by either the young people who are associated with gang activity, their parents, or community leaders who may hold views contrary to those promoted by the police. If news stories are the result of struggles among different social actors to promote a particular point of view, then the resources available to the police, as well as the lack of resources in communities in which organized baseball games for young people are out of reach, need to be considered in the evaluation of news stories about Mexican American youth gangs. Not only must access to resources be considered, but the cultural context must also be examined. As stated earlier, news production takes place within a cultural setting.

CULTURAL INFLUENCES

Besides access to resources, there are cultural factors that work in the police department's favor when newsworkers are preparing a story about Mexican American youth gangs. The most important factor is that the police are seen by members of society, including journalists, as the organization responsible for maintaining the social order. The cliché about a "thin blue line" between civilized society and mayhem best exemplifies our culture's attitude toward the police. The idea behind the "thin blue line" is that on one side of the "line" are the forces of order, reason, and justice. On the other side of the "line" are the forces of chaos, unbridled passion, and uncontrolled violence. To a large extent, this metaphor makes possible many of the other less obvious ways that the police can influence the Mexican American youth gang story. Fear of the loss of control over minority neighborhoods or the working class, of social breakdown, leads to support for the police department's efforts to control what are defined by mainstream society as deviant behaviors. Maintaining the "thin blue line" is seen by many middle-class citizens as essential in the stabilization of society.

However, while it is important to realize that the police enjoy community support and have considerable resources that they can use to provide information to reporters about Mexican American youth gangs, other persons and organizations, such as community group leaders, for example, may also make information about Mexican American gangs available to the news media. Such information may at times conflict with what the police department is telling the news media.

In contrast to the public image of Mexican American youth gangs as out-of-control youth, disrespectful of authority, and hell-bent on senseless violence, the police department is perceived as the enforcer of society's rules and regulations—its laws. The selection of recruits for the police academy, their training, uniform, and badge of authority, all contribute to the image of a professional organization carrying out its duties at the behest of the community. In this sense, the police are seen as a legitimate organization while the Mexican American gang is seen as illegitimate. Researchers have noted how the emphasis by the news media on government military forces as professionally trained to use violence in an efficacious manner helps to distinguish them from rebels or "gangs" whose use of violence is defined as "senseless" (Fiske & Hartley, 1978, pp. 41–47).

To maintain this professional image and carry out their duties, the police use their resources to promote themselves in the community. As stated earlier, among the resources available to the police is that they are professionals paid by the community to maintain law and order. There is no arguing against the advantage of having access to tax dollars for recruitment, training, and salaries. A steady flow of income allows for a stable organization that can be projected to grow and develop in stages over the course of many years. Part of that growth and development includes learning how to cope with the news media.

It must be kept in mind that, for reporters, asking for and accepting such information does have consequences. Seeking such information from the police leads to the tying of the reporter's work to that of police work. Such ties offer the police plenty of opportunities to influence the production of the Mexican American youth gang news story because they can provide or withhold information depending on whether or not the information itself, or the way it is presented to the public by television news reporters, suits their interests.

This ability to either make available or withhold information should not lead to the conclusion that the police have absolute or nearly absolute power to determine the form and content of Mexican American youth gang stories.

GETTING TO THE SOURCE

While it is common to argue that the police have tremendous influence in the production of crime news, such as news stories about Mexican American youth gangs, formulating theoretical explanations to support such a view has proved to be a difficult task. Some researchers have promoted the idea of "primary definers" to explain the role of the police in the reporting of crime and deviance (Hall et al., 1978). Primary definers are said to work within a social structure that gives them extraordinary influence in the production of news, especially crime news. In the case of the police and their relationship to crime news stories, this view at first appears a viable explanation for the reports about crime and deviance seen in the news media including local television news. The social identity of the police as the enforcement arm of society, the professionalization of police duties, and a willingness to work with the media to present their perspectives on crime and criminals to the public are three important reasons that support the view of the police as primary definers.

Critics of this view, however, have pointed out weaknesses in the explanatory power of the primary definer perspective of news production. One problem with the idea of primary definers, according to Schlesinger and Tumber (1994), is that it fails to explain who the primary definers are when there is a conflict among official sources. The argument for the idea of primary definers assumes a unified front on the part of police agencies. If one police agency, say the metropolitan police, is not in agreement with another police agency, for example, the sheriff's department, then who can be referred to as the primary definer in such cases?

Yet another source of conflict regarding the information being disseminated to the news media may originate with police officers themselves. That is, a police officer or officers may not agree with another officer or officers' views about the Mexican American youth gang situation. Such internal disagreements, while rare, do take place. Evidence of such a conflict, which is examined later in this chapter, was found in the police department of the city of Austin and its handling of the information it made available to the news media. The lack of agreement, and in some cases contradictory statements, among primary definers raises questions about this perspective.

Another point raised by Schlesinger and Tumber (1994) is that in instances when official sources ask to speak to reporters "off the record," the information they supply to the media cannot be attributed to them. In such cases, the argument for primary definers as having tremendous influence in the construction of crime stories is contradicted by the fact that the source remains anonymous.

Schlesinger and Tumber (1994) also point out that relationships between sources can change over time. There is evidence that the relationship between the news media and the police has undergone dramatic changes in the last thirty years. Specifically, the relationship has changed from an adversarial relationship in which the police were apprehensive about talking to the media, the "no comment" approach to dealing with the news media, to a more collegial relationship in which the police make every effort to get their take on issues before the public via the news media.

Perhaps the most troublesome aspect of the primary-definer explanation for crime news is that it paints the news media as passive in the production of news. As Schlesinger and Tumber (1994) argue, within the logic of the concept of primary definers "there is no space to account for occasions on which media may themselves take the initiative in the definitional process by challenging the so-called primary definers and forcing them to respond" (p. 19). Indeed, few researchers who study Mexican American youth gangs fail to acknowledge that the news media have contributed more to the hysteria about Mexican American youth than to reasoned discussion (McWilliams,

1990; Moore, 1991; Turner & Surace, 1956; Zatz, 1987; Vigil, 1988). While the idea of primary definers helps us understand the influence that the police have on the production of the Mexican American youth gang news story, it falls short in explaining the influences that are a result of the interaction of other persons and organizations on the production of the Mexican American youth gang news story.

Another view, closely aligned with the primary-definer model, explains the reliance on the police for information about Mexican American youth gangs as a result of the expectations society places on persons and organizations assigned to deal with certain matters. Becker (1967) refers to a "hierarchy of credibility" to explain how journalists turn to people in positions of authority for "expert" commentary on issues of the day. This hierarchy of credibility helps explain why police comments, observations, and recommendations for dealing with the Mexican American youth gang problem will, in certain circumstances, tend to carry more weight than those of the average citizen. The hierarchy of credibility is related to Hallin's (1994) view of experts, which he claims that in network news about political campaigns have become increasingly important (p. 137). Rather than journalists making statements to the public, experts are introduced to comment on the issue or issues being covered. Commentary from experts, however, is not a guarantee of objectivity and certainly not a guarantee of truth.

Researchers have long noted how the police can skew news stories about youth in general (Cohen, 1972; Ferrell & Websdale, 1996; Males, 1999; McWilliams, 1990; Miller, 1975, p. 1) and about Mexican American youth gangs in particular. Hagedorn (1998) writes that "the media forms and reinforces a law enforcement focus on gangs" (p. 24). Moore (1991), for example, notes that, contrary to the Los Angeles Police Department's information to the media about increased gang involvement in drug sales from 1983 to 1985, most of those arrested for drug dealing were not gang members (pp. 4–5). Vigil (1988), writing about gang language and clothing styles, explains that "Police officials have often viewed such creative cultural forms as representative of deviance. The media, especially newspapers, have followed a similar course in making dress styles a badge of dishonor" (p. 40). He goes on to explain that "because of police and media influences, the public has nevertheless tended to perceive such styles as reflective of criminal behavior" (p. 40).

These distortions about the Mexican American youth gang in the news media are partly the result of the relationship between the police and television news reporters. The police willingly provide information, while reporters usually take the information without question and present it to the public. Given the cultural values associated with the police and their role in society as protectors of the social order, it is almost impossible to question a reporter's efforts to get a police reaction to a drive-by shooting or some other criminal act thought to be related to Mexican American gangs. In fact, considering the cultural values involved, it makes sense that the police would be contacted by the news media. Ignoring police observations of such events would be seen as poor reporting by most consumers of television news. Indeed, "common sense" argues that police observations should be included in such reports.

According to the hierarchy of credibility theory, the police are sources of information for news stories about Mexican American youth gangs because they are recognized as legitimate authority figures responsible for maintaining the social order. The assumption, on the part of news reporters as well as the public, is that in a bureaucratically structured society, one can find individuals who are more qualified than others to respond to questions and explain events (Becker, 1967; Fishman, 1980, p. 51).

It is also important to note that this dependence on "experts" is part of the strategy of objectivity (Tuchman, 1978; Schudson, 1978). That is, reporters need to give air time to experts in order to avoid the accusation of bias. The ideal of objectivity demands that stories be free of the reporter's thoughts or feelings about an issue. The emphasis is on reporting the facts; however, reporters can convey their own thoughts or feelings by selecting experts with whom they agree. In this way, the illusion of objectivity in the news can be maintained.

As related in the previous chapter and reported by other researchers, such as Chibnall (1977), Ericson et al. (1989), Kaniss (1991), and Schlesinger and Tumber (1994), crime reporters tend to maintain close ties to police officers and the police department's public information office. Such connections are not new. Crime reporting has been traced back to the days of the penny press. Mott (1962) wrote that "Bad taste, coarseness which sometimes became indecency, overemphasis on crime and sex . . . were [the] outstanding sins of these newspapers" (p. 243).

Later, in the era of "yellow journalism," the same trend continued. Juergens (1966) described the strategy of Joseph Pulitzer in the development of yellow journalism: "Among the types of stories played up by the *World* in its early years were accounts of human sacrifice by religious sects in the United States, a description of unusual types of weapons used to commit murder, a story of canibalism at sea, and numerous accounts of sensational crimes" (p. 55, cited in Kooistra & Mahoney, 1999). As Emery, Emery and Roberts (1996) state "yellow journalism offered a palliative of sin, sex, and violence" (p. 194).

The latter-day version of this type of reporting, especially as it appears on television news, is referred to as "tabloid journalism" (Fiske, 1996, pp. 47-48 and Kooistra & Mahoney, 1999). Like news reporters in general, television news reporters have long known that they can depend on the police for material for stories. The need for visual material for television news has led to the observation that in local television news, form supersedes content. Local television news has come under attack from several researchers for reporting about sex and crime while ignoring economic, political, and social issues (Altheide, 1976). The term "Eyewitless News," a play on "Eyewitness News," to refer to local television news exemplifies many critics' opinions of local television newscasts. The introduction of the "happy news" format in the late 1960s and early 1970s (Hallin, 1987, p. 37) further reinforced the idea of television news as lacking in substance. Even within the profession of newswork there is a tendency for print journalists to look down on television news reporters. A newspaper editor I interviewed good-naturedly interrupted one of my questions about "broadcast journalists" with the question, "Isn't 'broadcast journalist' an oxymoron?"

Police departments, as in the days of the penny press and yellow journalism, continue to supply much of the information and imagery about crime for the mass media (Sanders & Lyons, 1995). The news media today, including local television news, have come to rely on local police agencies for information that can be used to produce news stories.

It is important to keep in mind that this dependence of the reporters on the police is not natural or otherwise preordained. There are other sources besides the police for stories and information that may make a good news story but which are not tapped by reporters as often as are the police. One reason is that the police not only have raw material for stories but they also know how to present it to reporters in a such a way that it can be easily packaged into a news story. Other sources of information about crime typically cannot match the police in terms of the type of material available for news stories, the consistency with which the material can be delivered, and the format in which the material is presented to newsworkers.

GETTING THE STORY OUT AND MEETING THE DEADLINE

Like the publishers and reporters in the days of the penny press and later the yellow press, today's television news reporters understand that the material for television news must appeal to the broadest audience possible. Stories about violence and deviance fall into this category. In addition, as mentioned earlier, the material provided by the police is often delivered to reporters in a manner that makes it fairly easy to mold into a television news story. In the city where this study took place in the early to mid 1990s, there was a conscious effort on the part of the police to work with the news media to get messages out to the public:

> This is a project we started a couple of years ago, how can we partner with the media to find mutual goals, why don't we work together to reduce the fear of crime. (Police Administrator, personal communication)

Such cooperation is related to changes in the political-economy perspective of newswork. As we learned in the previous chapter, in the era of "market-driven journalism" (McManus, 1994), television news reporters came under increased pressure to produce more stories. When such productivity pressures are coupled with deadline pressures, it becomes clear that one of the reasons why television news reporters find police information convenient to work with is that it reduces their time hunting for information as well as the time molding that information into a television news story. Understanding the pressures created by ratings and deadlines helps explain why reporters are ready to turn to the police for information for stories.

The obvious examples of such cooperation are the regular news series like *Crime Stoppers*, *Partners Against Crime*, and *Crime Watch*. In these series, the television news departments depend entirely on the police for material to fill two or three minutes of the news program.

An unsolved crime is reenacted and then viewers are asked to call the police if they have any information that may help the police close the case. A reward is offered to the viewer or viewers who supply information that leads to an arrest and conviction. According to police interviews, television stations are more than willing to provide airtime: "All the stations want to do something. The Department's got *Partners Against Crime* on one [station], *Crime Stoppers* on one, *Crime Watch* on the other one" (Police officer, personal communication).

Reporters are aware that the news program must attract a large audience if it is to be profitable. Closely related to profitability is keeping the cost of producing stories to a minimum. Production schedules and deadlines impose time limits on reporters that contribute significantly to the dependence on sources for material for stories. This dependence helps keep costs down since a reporter spends less time on a story. Gandy (1982) has written of how this system of providing information to reporters, what amounts to an "information subsidy," reduces the cost of producing stories.

A more independent approach to news story production would require more time for research and production. More time would be required for research because new sources, who might be able to expand the horizons of the story, would have to be found and interviewed. Production time would increase because new ways to tell the story would have to be found and incorporated into the visual and audio portions of the news story. Finally, more air time would be required because it would take longer to explain to the viewers why the new and different views are held by the new sources. For these financial and logistical reasons, reporters rely on a tried-and-true method for telling stories that is cost-effective in both time and money.

In this system of news production, the work of the reporter is not only related to prevailing assumptions and attitudes but also to how the police are organized to carry out their tasks and perform their duties. While such structural features of news reporting are important they are not as overriding as some researchers have believed (Fishman, 1980; Gans, 1980; Hall et al., 1978; Herman & Chomsky, 1988; Tuchman, 1978). While the organization of newswork and its impact on news production should not be overlooked, neither should it be privileged to the point where other factors are minimized or dismissed. Routines of news production and other structural features of newswork need to be considered when studying the production of news, but they need to be complemented by a broader scope of research that includes the influences of groups and organizations, as well as individuals, outside the newsroom.

ORGANIZING TO FIGHT CRIME

Another advantage that the police enjoy, already mentioned above, is that they have the backing of the community. In the eyes of the community, the police are professionals who investigate crimes and collect information about those crimes. This duty gives the police tremendous leeway in deciding which cases are investigated and which are placed lower down on the priority list. This in turn determines what gets reported by the news media and what gets buried in police reports.

While the police do not make laws, what the police choose to investigate and how they choose to investigate it are two strategies that can give them great influence in how crime news is reported by the news media, including television news. In an earlier chapter, we saw how initiation rites, including beatings, illegal use of alcohol and other drugs, and in some cases even murder can be labeled "gang" activity in one setting, such as a poor neighborhood with a high number of minority residents, or "youthful indiscretion" on a college campus with a large number of white, affluent students. In a college town, it is not unusual for some members of university fraternities, school organizations such as the band, and athletic teams to get involved in hazing incidents. Such behavior can involve minor infractions of the law, such as encouraging underage drinking, to major crimes, such as initiation rites that include beatings, rapes, and other forms of abuse, and in rare cases even murder. These crimes are typically committed by two or more persons who have identifying insignia or symbols. In other words, they could be considered a "gang" as legally defined by several states. Yet, unlike Mexican American youth who live in certain parts of town, these incidents are rarely reported as part of a growing pattern of behavior that calls for the formation of special police organizations such as an "anti-fraternity unit" or even an "anti-hazing unit."

Much, not all, of this labeling can be traced back to a law enforcement interpretation of events. For example, at the scene of a shooting, a police officer may suspect that a participant, or participants, in the shooting may be a member of a gang. The officer then relates his suspicions to a reporter who then includes in his news story that "Police believe the shooting may have been gang related" (6:00 P.M.

newscast, April 16, 1993). In another example, the television news reporter opened with the following narration over video of a neighborhood with a large Mexican American and African American population: "Last night there was no safety and security in being at home for Tom Kevin. His front yard became a statistic—another drive-by shooting that looks like right now to be gang related." No source was given by the TV reporter for such an assessment. No explanation of why the reporter was telling the audience that the incident was associated with gangs was provided. Attribution and explanation are not necessary in these reports. Both reporter and police, as well as viewers, understand that it is "common sense" that such incidents are "gang related." Such assessments have become so routine they are accepted as "true," and "factual."

CONTAINING THE FEAR OF GANGS

Common sense can become a burden for some police officers, especially those in the higher ranks. While the news media continue reporting about gang activity, police administrators may begin to feel the pressure from the community to solve the gang problem. Taxpayers may begin to think the police cannot handle the problem of gangs. In such a situation, the needs of the police begin to conflict with those of the television news departments. This seems to have happened in the city where this study took place. The police, especially top-level administrators, began to feel pressure from the citizens to do something about the gang problem. One technique was to quit mentioning "gangs" in information given to the news media.

> It got to a point that everything that happened, the first, and still today, the first question that is asked is, "is this gang related?" If you have a shooting that occurs in certain areas of town the first question asked by the media is, "is this a gang related incident?" We don't know, maybe, maybe not. If we say "maybe," "Police suspect that this may be a gang-related incident" is what you see . . . on the news. (Police Administrator, personal communication)

The gang theme can meet the economic and production needs of reporters but can also raise concerns among taxpayers about the police department's professional competence. Recall that after the afternoon shooting in the middle of downtown during rush hour, some citizens called the mayor's office to say that they were going to start arming themselves if the city didn't do something about the gang problem. Nothing terrifies the police more than an armed citizenry because this increases an officer's risk of being shot and killed while carrying out police duties. It became important for the police administration to take control of the gang situation. However, taking such control meant having to convince the rank and file officers to play down the gang theme. High level police administrators began encouraging officers to quit using the word "gang" when talking to the news media:

> What we have tried to work out with our community here . . . is to educate our officers to say, "we don't know [if it is a gang-related crime]. We think it may be but we're not certain." I tell my guys just don't mention the word gang. If it comes us up say "Beats me. I don't really care. I'm looking for a crime. Not a group." (Police Administrator, personal communication)

However, the gang theme was not being given up easily by the rank and file. Some police officers disagreed with such an approach. One of the officers in the gang unit said that he believes in letting people know that gang activity is taking place in the community:

> I've found that different details in our department, like our homicide detail and different people, really have a problem coming out and saying whether it is gang related or not. And, like, it's something taboo, using the word gang. If it's a gang-related crime it's a gang-related crime, and there shouldn't be any reason not to acknowledge that. But for some reason or other there seems to be a kind of taboo for some of our units to mention that. (Gang Unit Officer, personal communication)

Another officer, also with the Gang Unit, said that there was conflict between the police administration and the members of the Gang Unit about whether or not to report a crime as "gang related."

> Our Assistant Chief, and the state people, feel that just because John Doe is a gang member and he assaults his wife, is that gang related? You know? It shouldn't be gang related. But for intelligence purposes we need to know what John Doe is doing every day of the week because we can utilize that kind of information in a case preparation to let the judge know that John Doe had committed eighteen assaults. (Gang Unit Officer, personal communication)

Thus we see a struggle within the police department over how best to deal with reporting on gangs. On the one hand, there is a group that would like to see crimes reported simply as crime stories, period. The belief is that such an approach would minimize the fear of gangs and crime and help restore confidence in the police as a professional organization. Others believe that citizens have a right to know if gangs are active in the community. Advocates of this position tend to be members of the Gang Unit. Each group has its reasons for staking out a position on this matter. The important point is that the police department's approach to information it makes available to the news media about gangs is far from uniform, as the "primary-definer" theory argues (Hall et al., 1978, p. 57).

DEFINING GANGS

Providing information about Mexican American youth gangs to the news media is only one way that the police can influence the production of news stories about this group. In addition to having an office of public information that can provide reporters with material for stories, the police also make information available through workshops, conferences, and seminars.

At one point, the police department distributed information to schools and community agencies that defined a gang member as someone who wears certain color shoelaces or a Chicago Bulls jacket; even Mickey Mouse T-shirts were identified at one point as signs of gang involvement. Such porous definitions may be used by the police to conclude that an incident is the work of a gang or a gang member. Such a conclusion may then be related to reporters who tend to report in their stories, also without question, that the police believe a crime to be "gang related." The information in the news story has been attributed. It has been attributed to a "reliable" source, the police. Thus, according to good journalism practice, the reporter has carried out his or her duties in a professional manner. Yet the problem with the term "gang related" reflects much more than merely practicing "good journalism."

Once a decision about what to investigate and how to investigate it has been made, the police have access to a department that disseminates such information. A Public Information Office that deals with the community and the news media is one resource that gives the police a definite advantage when promoting policies or programs in the public sphere. In addition to its own police officers, who are encouraged to speak to the news media, and its own Public Information Office, the police have access to the personnel and information of other police departments and organizations. For example, the police department in the city where this research took place is in touch with the Federal Bureau of Investigation and police departments like the Los Angeles Police Department (Gang Unit Officer, personal communication; Police Administrator, personal communication). Work on gangs can be used to maintain close ties to other police departments. An officer with the Gang Unit said that officers regularly attend "Gang School":

> *Officer:* Everybody in our unit has gone to a gang school, [they go to] different places. I mean we got two that came back from Dallas last week, from being in a gang school.
>
> *Tovares:* What's a gang school?
>
> *Officer:* Well, they have gang conferences and schools that are set up throughout the country. We've sent some to different law enforcement agencies, different professionals in the field. . . . We've sent a couple to Anaheim, California, sent a couple to Tennessee, sent a number to San Antonio to gang school. And basically what it does is, it's a school just on gangs.

The officer went on to say that even his police department offered a one-day gang school, or what may be called a workshop. Officers from surrounding communities and even from cities hundreds of miles away attend. The one-day sessions focused on the different kinds of gangs in a community, the meaning of the colors worn by the gang members, the different signs used, "what to look for, how to attack the problem" (Gang Unit Officer, personal communication).

These conferences and workshops are not critical of what the police think and do about gangs but rather serve to *reinforce* what the police think and do about gangs. Equally as important is that they legitimize such thoughts and disseminate them among other police organizations and strengthen a network of antigang police officers. This kind of networking is beyond the organizational and financial resources of most neighborhood groups and community programs. Given such resources at their disposal, it would be a serious mistake to overlook the influence the police can have on the production of the Mexican American youth gang news story for local television news.

However, resources alone are no guarantee of a successful strategy for promoting a point of view on local television news. As the police administrator quoted above mentioned, circumstances beyond the police department's control may affect whether a story gets on the air.

The police, like others who contribute to the production of the Mexican American youth gang news story, do not work in a vacuum. Like reporters, the police work within a cultural setting. Such a setting includes the prevailing values, beliefs, and ideas of the community. These values and beliefs are shaped over time as a result of changes in economics, politics, and society. A short history of the development of the police department's Gang Unit can illustrate how these changes shape the strategies toward Mexican American youth gangs.

BRIEF HISTORY OF GANGS IN RESEARCH AREA

According to several police officers, the Antigang Unit had its roots in the Hispanic Crimes Unit, which was started in the mid 1980s when the city was undergoing a construction boom and builders were hiring laborers from Mexico. As one police officer said, "Man, back then this city was getting built by aliens. That's when they built all them buildings downtown. We had over a 100,000 [undocumented workers from Mexico] here" (Gang Unit officer, personal communication).

This construction boom was partly responsible for the development of the area of downtown known as Sixth Street. Sixth Street was a new, trendy, tourist-oriented area of town. The area known as Sixth Street borders a poor, minority neighborhood with a substantial Mexican American population known as East Austin. The neighborhood is separated from Sixth Street by Interstate Highway 35.

The Sixth Street area had been a vital part of downtown until the very late 1960s and early 1970s. By the late 1970s, the downtown area had become an older part of the city. The area was left with run-down warehouses and half-empty office buildings. Like many other urban areas in the late 1970s and early 1980s, Sixth Street was transformed from a part of downtown that had been abandoned by many businesses moving their operations to the suburbs into a fashionable, upscale strip of clubs and restaurants. The strategy of the officers patrolling the Sixth Street area became one of keeping young persons associated with hip-hop culture, including public dancing, away from Sixth Street, which was designed to attract affluent residents and tour-

Police Influence 121

ists. One of the first Mexican Americans hired by the police department (and who later started the Gang Unit) was involved in patrolling the Sixth Street area. He had volunteered for the walking beat that included Sixth Street in 1985. He recalled:

> *Officer:* We had those breakdancers back then, you know, coming up but that was just a group of kids.
>
> *Tovares:* Didn't clubs on Sixth Street complain about them?
>
> *Officer:* Oh hell yea. We had to run them out, you know. We finally cleaned them out. We got rid of them.
>
> *Tovares:* But they weren't really doing anything wrong?
>
> *Officer:* No. All they were doing was dancing in the middle of the sidewalk. But they didn't like it because they claimed, merchants claimed, that it was bad for their business because they [the breakdancers] were blocking doorways, stuff like that. They always find something. (Police Officer, personal communication)

An officer with the Gang Unit, who is white, had a different perspective on the problems on Sixth Street in the 1980s:

> Oh, probably '87, '88, '89, these kids would go down there and just stab people at random and this was part of their initiation, to stab somebody, to rob somebody, that was part of their initiation. (Gang Unit Officer, personal communication)

These two different perspectives on the presence of poor, young Mexican Americans in a trendy, new part of the city highlight the extent to which interpretations can distort the past. For the Mexican American police officer the teens and young adults were merely having fun. The number of persons attracted to these dance exhibitions interfered with customer traffic. No doubt fights broke out every now and then between dance groups. For the white officer, however, these adolescents were involved in serious violent and senseless crimes, such as random stabbings and robberies, as part of an initiation into a gang. On the one hand the Mexican American police officer remembers "just a group of kids." The white officer remembers a "gang": senseless violence, and random attacks, taking property, all for the purpose of being initiated into a gang. It was the latter perspective that took hold of the imagination of the affluent middle class, especially business owners along the Sixth Street area, who saw the young people as a hindrance to business and demanded that the police "run them out" of the area.

In order to build and develop the city, especially the downtown area, construction companies were heavily dependent on Mexican labor. Many of these construction workers were undocumented and, because of the possibility of deportation, were reluctant to put their money in banks. They tended to keep their money in their pockets. According to several officers, it was not unusual for some of these undocumented construction workers to walk around town with wads of $100 bills in their pockets.

> An organized group at that time, I believe, was a group called the Scorpions whose primary interest in life, in addition to fighting with gangs, was the robbing and killing of illegal aliens for their money, and at that time they all carried their money on them. (Police Administrator, personal communication)

Young men and adolescents from the area soon learned about these easy targets and began to attack these undocumented workers, especially on weekends when they were leaving neighborhood bars (Police Officer, personal communication). These attacks led to the formation of the Hispanic Crimes Unit to deal specifically with these robberies and murders.

During interviews it was apparent that several of the police officers and some members of the community felt uneasy about the term "Hispanic Crimes Unit." Many interviewees were quick to point out that the name did not indicate a special unit to target crimes committed by Latinos but rather referred to the undocumented workers who had been victimized by Mexican American and some African American adolescents and young men in the mid to late 1980s. Some of these groups of young men and adolescents became known to the police at this time, the most famous being a group of mostly Mexican Americans known as the Scorpions.

According to one police administrator, the crimes that the Scorpions were committing were "never considered a gang-related offense" (Police Administrator, personal communication). He went on to explain:

> We didn't categorize them as a gang-related offense. There were a group of people out here who were committing armed robberies and homicides. We didn't go into a lot of publicity about it. We just . . . went out

and did our job. The Chief was asked for a special task force for about three or four weeks and we had these Spanish officers and we went out and got State Senator Barrientos, who at that time was part owner in a Hispanic radio station, to go on the station and to ask the aliens to cooperate with us 'cause they were afraid we'd identify them and send them over to INS. (Police Administrator, personal communication)

The Hispanic Crimes Unit began to intensify its investigation. Several hundred persons, mostly adults, were arrested and sent to prison for robbery and homicides during this time. One tactic was to patrol the area of the city with the highest concentration of minority young people. Officers went out at night and took photographs of young people who were out late. When crimes were reported, the pictures were used to help identify perpetrators.

The kids were out till one o'clock in the morning [and we'd say] "Come here. What are you doing out here? How old are you? What's your name? Get over here." We'd take their picture. We put out information that anybody out after twelve [midnight] is going to get their picture taken by the police. Any kid out there under 17 years old. "We got your picture now go rob somebody." (Gang Unit Officer, personal communication)

According to one officer who worked on these cases, 313 adults, persons over 17, were sent to prison and three gangs were broken up as a result of the work of the Hispanic Crimes Unit. Not all of those persons were arrested for crimes against undocumented workers. The overwhelming majority of the arrests were for robberies and burglaries.

It was about this time that many persons working with the Hispanic Crimes Unit began to talk about a gang problem in the city. But their concerns fell on deaf ears.

You'd talk to someone here in town [and they would say] "No we don't have no gangs here. That's just in California." The schools, "Oh, no we don't have gangs here." Just real denial. (Gang Unit Officer, personal communication)

In the late 1980s, gangs, according to Hagedorn (1998, p. 23) were "discovered" by the media. The release of films like *Boulevard Nights* (1979); *Zoot Suit* (1981); *Colors* (1988); and later *American Me* (1992) and *Bound by Honor* (1993), contributed to this rediscovery. Newspapers, magazines, and television news began to focus on the topic of gangs. Locally, the news media began to ask questions about the gang situation. Initially, the police were not sure how to respond. This is because the city, like many other cities across the country, had previously communicated to the public that there weren't any gangs in the area. Most cities in the 1960s and 1970s did not admit to having a gang problem. As one police administrator said:

> You've got single parent families and these kids are out roaming the streets with nothing to do. All of a sudden they see this movie and this whole thing of gangs and banding together and doing all these great, crazy things and they started doing it. Well, the media started picking it up because about that time you had this wave of information coming out of California saying that we had a huge gang problem. Well the media here locally says, "how big of a gang problem do we have?" See? "Jeez, not much." "Well, how much is not much?" And so, they kept pushing. (Police Administrator, personal communication)

This example indicates that the news media, not the primary definers or "experts," decided to take on the issue of gangs. While television news reporters insist that they get their information from the police, which lends credence to the primary-definer role (Hall et al., 1978), in the above quotation a police administrator is placing responsibility for the coverage of gangs on the news media, including local television news.

Before the discovery of gangs by the news media, many crimes that would later become associated with gangs were reported only as homicides, robberies, and assaults. But by 1986 "crack," a new form of cocaine, was being sold in inner city neighborhoods in major metropolitan areas like New York, Miami, and Los Angeles (Mauer, 1999, p. 61). Crack, a kind of watered down cocaine, is a mixture of cocaine, water, and baking soda. This dilution made an expensive drug like cocaine affordable for less affluent drug users. As the national economy squeezed more poor and minority young people out of the job market the manufacture of crack provided an opportunity for some of these persons to earn money. The news media began paying attention to this new form of cocaine. As Mauer (1999) explains: "A media frenzy regarding the new drug developed by 1986, with much of the hysteria fueled by reports and information that later proved to be inaccurate" (p. 62). Stories about gangs and gang wars directly related to the sale of crack began to be featured in television news programs as well as other news media. As the hysteria about gangs swept across the county in the late 1980s, news media in Austin began asking the city police for information about gangs. What had gone unnoticed in the past became the focus of attention.

> Understand that we've always had gangs. Always have.... It is not something new.... I can remember as far back as the '70s when I was a patrol officer, of going to drive-by shootings, of the rivalry between a group and another group ... but until the late '80s and early '90s they didn't get a lot of attention, at least not in this area. Now they may have in Chicago, they may have in New York. (Police Administrator, personal communication)

Reporters began to ask the police about the extent of the gang problem in the city. They wanted to report about the gang problem in their community. They wanted to know if there was a gang problem. If so, how big of a problem was it? If not a big problem, the news media wanted to know whether the police were strategizing to contain it. New vocabularies began to develop to discuss the gang problem. Some cities were said to be in "denial" about their gang problem. Rather than facing the gang problem and taking it head-on, these cities were said to simply deny that a gang problem existed.

Another group challenged such perceptions. In cities smaller than Los Angeles, Chicago, or New York, some community leaders began to speak about an "emerging" gang problem. This term suggested that a city or town with a small gang problem could find itself with a full-blown gang problem on its hands if some strategy of containment were not developed. Austin was said by many to have an "emerging" gang problem (Gang Unit Officers, personal communication).

At the forefront of the "emerging gang city" argument in Austin were two Mexican American police officers who were working with young people primarily in the downtown area and east side of the city. As members of the Hispanic Crimes Unit that had been started in the mid-1980s to investigate the beatings and deaths of undocumented workers, these two officers had contact with the Latino community. One of these officers had achieved state recognition for his service to the community. The officer, a Mexican American and native of Austin, was the most decorated officer in the state. He had joined the force in 1967 when the police department had only four Hispanic officers out of 400 officers. Much later, this officer would be asked to join the Hispanic Crimes Unit. It was as a member of this unit that he began to deal directly with what would later become recognized as gangs.

> I didn't want to go [to the Hispanic Crimes Unit]. I was happy where I was [walking a beat in downtown]. They told me "c'mon, its only for ninety days." And I went and I ended up staying for four years. I wound up developing my own gang unit. (Gang Unit Officer, personal communication)

It was in the Hispanic Crimes Unit that this officer began working with another policeman. Their approach to dealing with the "emerging gang problem" was to make their presence in the community known. They worked at one of the police department's Neighborhood Centers.

In September 1993, the Street Crimes Unit and the Hispanic Crimes Unit were brought together to form a new Gang Unit. Prior to this, both the Street Crimes Unit and the Hispanic Crimes Unit handled gang crimes. The problem according to some observers is that the approach to gangs was not professional.

The Hispanic Crimes Unit had always been a high-profile unit. According to one administrator members of this unit would work mostly at night and "go to gang locations, try to catch them in a crime, try to get out there and what they call 'jack 'em up,' mingle with them, that sort of thing." He went on to explain some of the problems with this approach:

> There's no way you can go out there in a high-profile capacity, it's kind of a hit or miss thing, you know, you hope that you'll be out there, the ideal situation would be that you hope you'd be out there riding around, someone does a drive-by shooting, you hear the shots, you get behind the car that's responsible, get them stopped, get the perpetrators arrested, get your case worked up. But that's more fantasy than it is reality. All the major studies that have been done on police work show that the random patrol is really a waste of money. It really doesn't accomplish anything. (Police Administrator, personal communication)

The change was not an easy one. The officers who believed in the high profile approach did not want their duties changed. Although none of the officers I spoke with commented on tape, one supervisor did say, "One of the things we worked out is we took the two units and mixed up personnel, ah, and there were several reasons for this and I won't get into that, but we mixed up personnel and then we put them in an investigative capacity." Later, while escorting me to my car, the supervisor confided that he could not talk on tape about some officers who had complained about the changes in their duties. These officers felt that their high-profile police work was paying off.

The two Gang Unit officers also began to give talks at schools and community groups about the gang situation in the Austin area. The officer who had started the Gang Unit had become used to the spotlight. As one of the first Mexican American police officers in the department and as a hard-working investigator, he had received media attention in the past. "Everywhere I go I get a lot of publicity, the limelight. When you bust a lot of cases you make the news," he explained (personal communication).

His partner, on the other hand, was seeking publicity. It was about this time that the officer seeking publicity started to develop the idea of using rap music to reach young audiences with messages about the dangers of drugs and gangs. It was an idea that would eventually lead to the establishment of a stage act. The idea of rapping police officers was not unique. Other police officers in police departments in major metropolitan areas were trying new ways to reach young people with antigang and anti-drug messages. In Chicago, for example, three officers assigned to the Cabrini-Green area formed a rap group. The three officers, known as the Slicks or the Slick Boys, started performing in the 1990s (Avril, 1993; Terry, 1992). In the late 1980s in San Antonio, Texas, the San Antonio Police organized a rock and roll band to play at "Just Say No" rallies.

The rapping police officer became a celebrity in the community. Both he and his partner were in demand by grade schools, churches, parent groups, and community service organizations. The theme of their presentations—stay away from gangs and drugs—their status as police officers, and the unique style of presenting their message—personal testimony and rap music—made them a hot ticket.

RAPPING AGAINST GANGS

The police department's Gang Unit was featured on the program *Top Cops*. Two officers in the Gang Unit were flown to Toronto, Canada, where the episode was filmed. They were introduced at the beginning of the *Top Cops* segment as two officers attempting to stop a "gang war" in Austin, Texas. The episode was very loosely based on a shooting incident in the downtown area. The actual incident was covered by the local news media as well as CNN and other network news services. As one of the members of the Gang Unit said during an interview "That incident put this city on the map." Producers for *Top Cops* who had seen the report about the shooting at Fifth and Congress contacted the two officers in the Gang Unit about the episode. The episode made the two police officers in the police department's Gang Unit local celebrities.

One of the officers of the Gang Unit had been trying to launch an acting and singing career. He had developed an act that he performed before students in school gymnasiums and at antigang and "Just Say No" rallies. According to his own promotional materials, he was available for rallies, workshops, and conferences. At these events, the officer would sing his own rap composition about the dangers of gangs and drugs while dressed in his police uniform and dark sunglasses. Local television news reporters I spoke with during the course of my research all commented positively on his act. At the end of the *Top Cops* episode that featured the shooting at a downtown street corner, the officer is seen on a crowded street corner rapping his antigang lyrics as a young black boy of about ten or eleven comes out of the crowd and starts dancing to the beat.

The routine was developed by a police officer while working as part of the police department's Gang Unit. An aspiring actor, the officer began to use performance art as a way to connect with students when invited to speak by principals and parent organizations about the dangers of gangs, violence, and drugs. Rap music, jokes, and his own personal story about growing up poor in the city's oldest Mexican American neighborhood, but determined to be successful, made up the performance. This character allowed the officer to get up on stage and perform before a live audience. The officer also had hopes of breaking into show business with his rap video, which was produced while he was on location in Toronto, Canada, working on the reenactment of the shooting at a downtown street corner. The rap video was rejected by MTV.

The same officer had produced an antigang poster campaign, which consisted of several posters that could be seen in restaurants, community centers, and schools in the area. Even some of the local theaters projected slides of the posters on the screen between film screenings. The black and white posters depicted images of gang activity accompanied by a phrase or statement designed to make young persons think about the negative consequences of joining a gang. In 1991, television public service announcements (PSAs) warning against gangs were also produced by the police officer. The message of these PSAs, which featured the two gang liason officers and a state senator, was "Say no to street gangs; say yes to your future." They were aired by local television stations in the television market and on public access channels.

These experiences with media gave the Gang Unit a tremendous advantage when dealing with local television news reporters. The performances and presentations about the dangers of joining gangs, the poster campaign, and television spots made the members of the Gang Unit local stars. They became familiar with the members of the news media. There was a personal relationship between the reporters and the officers of the Gang Unit. While performing on stage, the rapping police officer was providing visual material for the newscast. The officers, after repeated interactions with the news media, became articulate spokespersons who could give reporters sound bites and statements that could easily fit into the local television news format.

This brief description of how two officers in the police department's Gang Unit used media to create awareness about the city's "gang problem" is an example of how the police can use their status in the community and information to influence the production of the Mexican American youth gang story for local television news. This use of information is related to the police department's role as a legitimate organization with the responsibility of maintaining the social order and promoting prosocial values in young persons.

As we have seen in this and the previous chapter, newsworkers are dependent on the police for information about criminal activity. Using such information without question can lead to distortions that are reported as fact. Such a case seems to have occurred when the police made information about the number of gangs in the community available to the news media.

Reporters, as we learned in the last chapter, insist that information about gang-related crimes comes from the police. Police, however, insist that they provide the news media with a full explanation of the gang data but that reporters refuse to report the story behind the gang numbers and "gang-related" incidents. One police officer said in an interview:

> A lot times people say, "well, it shouldn't be gang-related stats unless you can prove that he did this because he is a gang member, to better himself as a gang member, or he tells you in the interview that it was part of a gang initiation, and/or in your interviewing this individual he tells you that four of five of us gang members got together and we were needing money for the gang so we went out and did all these robberies." And some people's argument is that just because John Doe is a gang member and he holds up eighteen 7-Elevens this month—is that

gang related? Well, we track it as gang activity. (Gang Unit Officer, personal communication)

According to some police officers, the news media simply refuse to give the explanation behind the term "gang-related incident." Officers who deal with the news media explained that all of the information for an accurate count of gang members in the city is made available to the news media. Time is taken to explain to the news media how the gang numbers are calculated, yet many believe that the news media do not give the entire explanation. Officers explained that the news media are selective of the numbers associated with gang activity. The reporters select only the information that suits their needs and ignore information that will detract from the impact of the story, such as the number of defunct or inactive gangs. In this case, it is the information reporters decide to leave out that contributes to the perceptions of a "growing" or "out of control" gang problem.

ORGANIZING TO FIGHT GANGS

By making a conscious effort to organize antigang units and go after gang members and bust up gangs, the police to a large extent are defining crime and criminals for the media. This is demonstrated in how the gang problem ebbs and flows. In the 1930s and 1940s, much attention was paid to youth gangs and the Mexican American gang problem. In the 1950s and 1960s, that attention subsided. Then, in the late 1970s and early 1980s, the attention was again focused on youth gangs with Mexican American youth caught up in the hysteria. However, we have seen how crime among adolescents and young adults has been stable over decades. There is also evidence that most of the arrests for drug dealing and possession are of young men who are not members of gangs (Moore, 1991). The Zatz (1987) study also showed how most arrests of "gang" members were for noncriminal acts, like fighting or being out after curfew. Zatz also pointed out that by organizing an antigang unit, the police in Phoenix focused on Mexican American youth behavior. Such surveillance led to increased arrests in that demographic group not because of increased gang activity but rather because of the social perception, or cultural expectation, that Mexican American youth must be involved in gangs. By playing into the cultural expectations, the police influence the production of Mexican American youth gang stories.

This ability to contribute to how the media frame an issue like crime in the Mexican American community as "gang related" is tied to how the police carry out their tasks and their relationship with the news media. Like most of everyday life, the police carry out their daily tasks in an environment that does not invite questions. Not only are questions from television news reporters discouraged by the structure of newswork but so too are questions about crime in general. What constitutes a crime, who makes the laws that define a crime, who is determined to be a criminal, and other matters relating to the mundane duties of police officers rarely come up in conversations with police officers. These matters are accepted by the police as a given. Crime is what the law says it is and police officers are ordered to carry out their duties according to the law. The larger questions about what the law is, who makes it, and for what purpose are not discussed by police officers, at least not with researchers. This is important because by not questioning basic premises of law enforcement, police officers can convince themselves that what they are doing is "objective" and "good," something common sense tells them is a service to the community. Of course, as we saw in the introductory chapter, common sense is a form of communication that reinforces the position of the powerful and wealthy.

Along these same lines, the police officers I interviewed never questioned the definition of gangs. In fact, most police officers, including those in the police department's Gang Unit, could not provide the legal definition of a gang. While all police officers interviewed assume that gangs exist, that it is their job to stop gang members from engaging in criminal activity, and that they should break up gangs, none could provide a definition of a gang. In fairness, the police I interviewed knew that the state had legally defined a gang, but none could articulate even a vague notion of that legal definition. This lack of a clear understanding of what constitutes a gang sets up a variety of minority youths and young adults in different situations to be thought of as a gang by the police.

> I've been in this business long enough that I can drive down the street and I see a group of kids and it's just a group of kids riding around together and I see another one, and that group of kids is looking for trouble. They're all wearing the same kind of baseball cap, they're all wearing them in the same way, they've all got red bandanas on, that sort of thing. It's pretty obvious. (Police Officer, personal communication)

It is precisely this kind of attitude, within a cultural context that includes a history of racism, that leads seamlessly to what has come to be called "racial profiling," meaning that members of minority populations are targeted by the police for harassment not because of anything they have done but because of a piece of clothing, the color of a bandana, or the color of their skin.

CONCLUSION

Like the news media and newsworkers, the police also operate in a cultural environment. While there is little doubt that the police do help maintain the social order, equally certain is that embedded in their role are the values, beliefs, and ideas of the time, including racist and class values and beliefs. These values and beliefs are manifested on a daily basis in police work. Racial profiling, holding and questioning young Mexican Americans on "suspicion" of illegal activity, even beating and in rare cases shooting them are all indications that the police are expressing the racism in society in their daily activities.

We can be sure that there are persons in any community who will not hesitate to intimidate, hurt, and even kill others if it suits their needs. However, when an entire category of persons, such as young Mexican American males, are ascribed such traits in the local media while young affluent white males are rarely, if ever, presented in such a context, then another line is crossed, a line that gives individuals respect and dignity based on their behavior and not their skin color or social class.

While in the past the police have been blamed for creating the "gang problem" (McWilliams, 1990; Gonzales, 1981), the truth is that while the police exert tremendous influence over how the media and the community will perceive Mexican American youths, they, like reporters, operate within a cultural context that reinforces their thinking and behavior regarding Mexican American youth gangs. The history of the reporting on Mexican bandits and gangs in the news media (see chapter 2) illustrates the role of the police in such matters. As symbols of law and order, the police, including sheriffs and school district security officers, are expected to clamp down on minorities and "keep them in their place." Within such a setting, it should not be surprising that an attitude of "us versus them" has developed between the police and Mexican American youth.

When news reporters need information about youth gangs quickly, sometimes within a couple of hours, they know that they can depend on members of the Gang Unit to return calls and provide a usable sound bite. They also know that they can count on the police department's Public Information Office to provide "statistics" and other information on the gang problem. This accessibility is partly the result of a news production routine adhered to by television crime news reporters.

These examples clearly show how the police actively contribute to the news media's perception of an increase in gang membership, the increase in the number of gangs, and the image of well-organized gangs. The contributions from the news media, including local television news, also fuel the illusion that gangs are a growing problem.

Chapter 5

Community Leaders

> There are a handful of folks out there who seem to have a personal agenda and a desire to keep the issue of gangs on the forefront of the media.
> —Police Administrator, personal communication

Newsworkers and the police are not the only ones contributing to the production of the Mexican American youth gang news story on local television news. Another group of persons contributing to the production of such stories is community leaders. Community leaders are usually associated, either directly or indirectly, with social service organizations. These organizations tend to be resource-poor, that is, they tend to be underfunded, understaffed, and short on technology when compared with local television news departments, the police department, and other organizations associated with the criminal justice system. Lack of resources is the primary reason community leaders are at a distinct disadvantage when attempting to make their voices, and the views of their organizations, heard via local television news. However, this is not the only reason. Values and perceptions about the gang problem that are different from those of newsworkers and affluent television news consumers are also reasons why some organizations find themselves cropped out of the television news stories about Mexican American youth gangs.

Persons associated with a community organization attempt to get the attention of local television news because it is a good way to showcase the programs and activities sponsored by the organization. Such coverage serves as a public relations effort. The television news viewer gets to see what the organization is doing and how it is contributing to the betterment of the community. This promotion and public relations strategy also help in the agency's efforts to secure funds from government bodies and private foundations. Often the first step to receiving funds is to establish a positive public presence. Local television news can be a valuable resource for achieving such a goal.

Not all persons addressing the gang situation on local television news seek attention for a community organization. Some individuals expressing concern about the gang situation in Mexican American communities may simply be seeking media attention for themselves. As the quote at the beginning of this chapter points out, some persons' interest in the gang situation may be less than noble. Some persons, especially those contemplating running for public office, were often accused by some members of the community of using the gang issue to keep their names before the public.

In the following pages I delineate how these community leaders and organizations can influence the Mexican American youth gang news story. However, as this brief introduction has highlighted, the approaches and views of the leaders and organizations involved with youth gangs are not always similar and may even be contradictory. Some leaders and organizations accept the prevailing views and opinions about the Mexican American youth gang. Others reject the prevailing views and propose new and different ways of looking at the issue of Mexican American youth gangs. How these different individuals and organizations with different agendas and views interact with television newsworkers and the police in order to influence the production of the Mexican American youth gang news story is examined next.

DEFINING COMMUNITY LEADERS

One problem when studying the influence of community leaders on Mexican American youth gang news stories is that community leadership is difficult to define. Some leaders seek the attention of the media while others do not. Some leaders are sought out by the media for an on-air comment while others are not. Some who seek attention may not necessarily get it, while some who may not particularly seek media attention may find themselves at the center of the media's gaze.

Some community leaders interviewed for this study reported that they were able to establish a relationship with local television news stations. Others complained that their efforts to get television coverage of their organization and its activities were ignored.

Leaders may be persons elected to positions of authority, such as president or spokesperson for a neighborhood organization, or may be appointed by an elected official, such as the mayor or governor. Typically the appointments are to committees or boards assigned to investigate the extent of the gang problem in the community and make recommendations about how to solve it.

Elected officials usually do not have a problem getting access to the news media. In fact, the news media almost cater to their need to communicate with the citizens. When a city council member, county supervisor, or state legislator calls a press conference, the news media, including local television news, are very accommodating. Elected officials, for the most part, mirror the views and ideas about gangs that are found in the communities that elected them. In the course of my research on Mexican American youth gangs and local television news, I never came across an elected official who contradicted mainstream thinking about gangs.

Besides being elected or appointed, community leaders may also be created by the news media. For example, one woman whose son was shot in what the news media reported as a gang-related shooting became someone the news media called on for comments when subsequent shootings took place. This woman later told me during an interview that her son had told her that he had not been shot by a rival gang member but by the mother of a rival gang member. She never revealed this information to the police or the news media. Soon after her son had been shot, she announced that she was forming her own organization called Mothers Against Gangs. According to her, reporters called her for interviews and offered to help her in any way that they could.

Leaders may also be sought by a television station to help with its overall coverage of minority communities. One television station had appointed an advisory board to meet with station management several times a year and provide comments and suggestions about how to best serve the Latino community. Some members of this advisory board, however, had begun to criticize the advisory board as mere "window dressing." They claimed that the station was using the advisory board as a prop to deflect criticism of its coverage of the Mexican American community, which some said had not changed since the board had been assembled. While I was interviewing one religious leader in the Mexican American community, he received a call from the station telling him of an upcoming meeting. He responded, while I sat in his office, that he would be resigning from the advisory board because he had not seen any progress in the coverage of the Latino community since the formation of the television station's advisory board.

In this book, the term "community leaders" refers to persons who may be regularly sought by the news media to make statements about gang-related matters. Ex-gang members may find themselves called upon to give their views on such topics as the extent of gang membership in the city, a shooting, a new social service program, or a change in policy such as the introduction of a teen curfew. One ex-gang member made several appearances on local television news because of his antigang presentations around town. He frequently spoke at grade schools and high schools and often testified before city council and county supervisors in favor of more funding for antigang programs.

Depending on the issue and the availability of other sources, almost anyone may find themselves as a spokesperson for the community. A school principal or teacher, social worker, or—although it is rare—a Mexican American teenager may be approached by a television news reporter for a sound bite. A parent may be asked to comment on what the city or state might do to help curb the neighborhood gang problem. In such a role these persons often become advocates for either more funding for programs and other resources for the community, or for harsher treatment of young offenders by the police and the courts.

Police officers who are working after hours, such as the police officer from the previous chapter who performed his rap music before children and teens, may also be considered community leaders at times. If they take on a different persona such as a rapping police officer and perform during off-duty hours they may be considered community leaders rather than police officers. So while the lines that distinguish a community leader are not always clearly drawn it can be said that there are persons who either seek the news media or are sought by the news media in order to make public comments and offer opinions on the gang situation in the community. Often these persons, either intentionally or by default, take on an aura of leadership after they have appeared on a local television newscast.

While almost anyone may find himself or herself cast by local television news as a spokesperson or community leader, holding on to that role requires work. An examination of local television news reveals that certain community leaders are regularly contacted by the news media for comments on the Mexican American young gang situation. Discussions with persons who make frequent appearances on local television news to comment on the gang situation reveal that their presence on the screen is the result of consistent efforts to get the attention of television news reporters and producers.

IMPORTANCE OF STUDYING INFLUENCE OF COMMUNITY LEADERS

It is important that we study the role of community leaders as influences on the Mexican American youth gang story for local television news because other researchers who have studied the impact of individuals and organizations on the news-making process (Goldenberg, 1975; Tuchman, 1978; Gitlin, 1980) have pointed out that not all individuals and groups have equal access to the news media. This is a central issue in a study of the influences on the production of the Mexican American youth gang news story because those persons who are given access to television viewers can skew information in one direction or another. Several researchers (Dorfman & Schiraldi, 2001; Males, 1999; Hagedorn, 1998) have documented a tilting in the selection of sources for stories about juvenile crime in favor of a criminal justice perspective. For example, we saw in the previous chapter how the police tend to promote a "criminal justice" perspective on the Mexican American youth gang news story. We also saw in Chapter 3 how television newsworkers can be absorbed by the police and its system of information production and dissemination. It is important to learn how community leaders gain access to local television news and what resources are available to them so that they can present their views on the Mexican American youth gang to the public.

In the past, different ethnic and minority groups have expressed concerns about being shut out from the news-making process and therefore silenced by the mainstream media. Generally speaking, being shut out of the news-making process means two things. The first is not being hired to work in television news. Being excluded from the newsroom meant that the news would continue to be presented from a white perspective, as the Kerner Commission (1968) pointed out decades ago and as subsequent reports have continued to point out (U.S. Commission on Civil Rights, 1977 and 1979). The second way of being shut out is to leave minority voices out of the pool of sources available for comments about news events. Women, African Americans, Latinos, and other groups have argued that tapping white males as sources for stories concerning women, African Americans, Latinos, and other groups denies members of these groups the opportunity to speak for themselves and present their views directly to the public. Thus the selection of persons to serve as sources of information for news stories is believed to influence how the story is presented on two levels. First, sources deliver information to the audience and in this way are able to influence the tone or perspective of a story. They are seen as persons knowledgeable about an issue and, in this sense, as "experts." When persons from outside the community serve as sources or spokespersons, the impression is created that the community is incapable of articulating its own problems. Second, some researchers have argued that when those being covered are overlooked as sources, they come to be seen as persons who are incapable of solving their own problems. Indeed Wilson and Gutiérrez (1995) refer to much of the coverage of minority communities as a "problem people" news frame, that is, a community that either makes problems for itself or for the larger society. Letting persons in the community speak to their own issues gives them the opportunity to define their own problems and propose their own solutions.

These questions and issues are important because they go to the heart of debates about the role of the news media in a democracy. As envisioned by the writers of the Constitution, especially the First Amendment, which protects freedom of speech and of the press, the purpose of the news media in a democracy is to make information available to the electorate. Such information can then be debated among the citizens who set policy either directly, by voting on certain proposals, or indirectly, by electing representatives who vote on proposals. According to the theory of the marketplace of ideas, in the process of these debates, persons begin to look beyond their own selfish, short-term interests and come to see how certain decisions can benefit the entire community in the long term. In colonial times, the marketplace of ideas was seen as a way of promoting the common good. Today it can be argued that ignoring information about Mexican American youth gangs or skewing information about this issue in a certain direction can mean that viewers are being denied access to information about a topic that is important to the future well-being of our society. The importance of studying how individuals become spokespersons for their communities is related to the need for information in a democratic society and the right of communities to articulate their own problems and needs as well as propose solutions for their problems and strategies for meeting their needs. In this way citizens feel that they have a voice in public debates and can engage in discussions with other groups and organizations. Studying how one gains access to local television news for the purpose of making statements and offering opinions about the Mexican American youth gang is a study in the relationship between communication and the democratic process.

This chapter examines how individuals can become spokespersons for their communities, who these spokespersons tend to be, and how they might influence the Mexican American youth gang news story.

GETTING MEDIA ATTENTION

There are two broad categories of community leaders when it comes to local television news stories about Mexican American youth gangs: those who get the attention of the news media and those who don't. Those who manage to get media attention for themselves and their organization over a period of time are pro-active. They take the initiative and contact the news media and make efforts to cultivate relationships with newsworkers. One community leader said that he and his group actively sought out reporters who would be willing to help them produce stories about the organization's efforts to wipe out graffiti and control the gang problem. On one occasion, he called one of the local television stations to notify the news director that he and a group from the neighborhood were going to try and catch graffiti artists in the act of spray-painting a wall. At the time, graffiti was a topic very much in the news, not only locally but nationally as well (Ferrell, 1996, p. 12).

> I called [a news manager] from channel X and told him, "hey, look, myself, the officer from our neighborhood police station, we are planning on doing a graffiti sting and we would like to know if you would like to send out a reporter to cover the story." And they sent a reporter. And we staked an area out at First and Wallace streets. And we got there about 9:30, 10 o'clock, I think it was, and set the camera up. (Community leader, personal communication)

Spending time with the reporter and photographer while waiting for someone to come and start spray painting the wall was an opportunity for everyone involved—community leader, police officer, reporter, photographer—to talk and get to know one another. This time allowed for a reporter-source relationship to develop. A big plus was that the "sting" was successful, someone did show up with intentions of spray painting the wall. The news team's camera caught the graffiti artists in the act. As a result, the reporter and the station did not feel that their efforts had been in vain.

> [We] started talking to one another and found out that we had [a lot in common]. We [developed] a real good relationship. We caught somebody that night, actually. On tape! They filmed it and everything. I mean it really caught the city by storm. And from that point on they figured "hey, this guy knows what he's doing out there." And the relationship was there. Me and [that reporter] went on to do a few, quite a few other stories, maybe about eight. Eight more stories of different issues of, ah, gangs in particular. (Community leader, personal communication)

From the point of view of the community leader and the news station, the sting operation was a success. That success led to more stories. Thus, in this case, the efforts by the community leader paid off.

Another community leader said that he and his neighborhood organization approached all of the news media in town, television news, newspapers, and radio, about their efforts to take back control of their neighborhood from the gangs. They explained to the local news media how they had long-term plans to turn the neighborhood around. Over several years, the neighborhood had acquired a reputation as an area in decline. Previously owner-occupied homes had been sold as a result of bankruptcy and turned into low-rent or subsidized housing under a government program known as Section 8. According to this community leader, only the local daily newspaper and two of the television stations responded positively.

> There was a time we had already sat down with all the different stations. In terms of media I have to tip my hat to two stations and the [local newspaper]. We said, "Look, this is what we want to try to do and we need your help." . . . They said they would help as much as they can. They were there for us. (Personal communication)

This neighborhood organization had a reputation among newsworkers for knowing how to deal with the news media. They were respected by newsworkers. Initially the leader of this group was just seeking media attention.

> No matter that there were negatives about the community or there were positives, at this point we didn't care, because what we wanted to do was bring the attention out to the community and let them know that we were involved. I was trying to put my face in every newscast and every, every time spot that they allowed me to. (Personal communication)

The strategy worked. The residents of the neighborhood he was trying to organize began to attend meetings and get involved in the organization. As a result of the media coverage, including local television news, political leaders began to take notice of the organization as well.

The point about not caring whether the news media were providing positive or negative coverage is important in this context. When asked for an example of media coverage that was negative, this community leader provided the following story in which a confrontation between three male African American teenagers and an older Mexican male escalated into a shooting after his truck came to a stop in the middle of the road, thus blocking the road. Not being able to get around him, the three African American teenagers started to honk their horn and curse the older driver. The incident had happened about three years before the interview took place.

> The guy pretty much couldn't understand half of what they were saying, but he knew something was going on. Well, all of a sudden, while the guy is moving, getting his truck out of the way, two shots rang out. And the kids took off and went to their house. Which happens to be right in front of my house. (Personal communication)

This incident happened close to 10:00 P.M., just as the community leader and his wife were getting ready for bed. They heard the gun shots and jumped out of bed. He went to his front door and walked outside to see what was happening. While he was outside the older Mexican gentleman in the truck drove up and asked this leader if he had seen three African American teenagers. The community leader responded that he didn't know what was going on and had just come out to see what was happening. As the older gentleman was starting to get into his truck, he noticed the three African American teenagers start to come out of one of the houses. The teenagers turned and went back inside. The community leader went on to describe what happened next.

> The Hispanic guy backs his car up after seeing them and starts to drive into their driveway where the car that they were in at the time they were messing with him is parked at. And the Mexican guy hits their car, I mean rear-ended that car so hard, and really it's one of these '76 Cutlass Supremes, I mean hard, big old tanks, I mean he left nothing to that car, nothing. He hits that car about two times and the three black guys come out with a gun and shoot about eighteen rounds. I mean they were trying to kill this guy. They didn't hit him. I mean this guy was so lucky, I mean twice, twice in less than an hour, this guy is shot at and not hit.
>
> By that time you know, police, everybody is coming, ah, the kids run inside and everything. By that time, you know, all the [television] stations went out there. I mean, everybody was out there. But the media portrayed it as a gang shooting, which it actually wasn't. It was three brothers, or three friends, with an argument with this other guy. The media portrayed it as a gang-related shooting, which it never was. But we said fine, let's leave it alone, because we knew there was a, behind that there was a lot more problems, and gang-related problems, that we needed to address. (Personal communication)

The leaders of the neighborhood organization were not sure if the three young men did or did not belong to a gang. The neighborhood did have a reputation of being a gang area: "We didn't know if these three kids were involved in a gang or not, because [the neighborhood] is known for a very well-known gang in the eastern part of the city known as the Dove Springs Posse, an African American gang, that is controlled by a Mexican American." The logic behind the organization's strategy seemed to have been that, since the neighborhood had gangs, it was all right not to challenge the news media in its reporting of a "gang-related" incident. The possible long-term benefits from such reporting outweighed the short-term negative publicity.

So we said, hey, you know, let's use this to go to the city, to go to the police department to say, "look, these are the things that are happening out here." I mean, we were trying to bring a community back that had no services, no clinics, no recreation facilities, nothing, you know, this was something, even though we used it as a tool, we used it as a tool to get some of the things that we've been getting in our community. It was something that happened. We didn't make it happen. What we did was, even though the media made it seem like a gang-related shooting, we said, OK, let's leave it at that. We didn't challenge that, because we knew that we had a bigger problem than just that shooting that was non-gang-related, but which was the gangs in the communities, the Dove Springs Posse, the Outlaws, OZ's, Latin Kings, you know, all of these gangs exist out there.

In this case, a shooting that was not gang related was interpreted as such by the news media and the police. Community residents did not discourage this media frame but instead welcomed it as an opportunity. They saw the gang theme as a way to get the city's attention. The gang theme could also be used when approaching city leaders for resources for the community. Improved street lighting, a police substation, health facilities, and a swimming pool and recreation center were argued as essential for the neighborhood if the fight against gangs was to be successful.

This neighborhood group used the gang theme to secure needed services for the community. They allowed misinformation, which the news media did not question because it did not violate the cultural expectations of newsworkers and viewers, to be used in news stories. In the long run, it allowed the news media to combine the gang theme with the success story, since the neighborhood was later said to be making a comeback. Thus, two of the news media's favorite themes—gangs and success—were combined in the reporting of this neighborhood. Television news stories reported that better lighting, increased police patrols and, much later, a new swimming pool were all signs that the people of the neighborhood had succeeded in taking back their neighborhood from the gangs. Many of these developments, especially the opening of the new pool, were "unveiled" with the news media in mind. Political leaders, city officials, and neighborhood residents were all invited. The community leaders of this particular neighborhood felt that they had succeeded in getting media coverage of their efforts to improve the neighborhood.

The leaders made themselves visible to their neighbors via the news media, especially local television news. Initially they allowed either positive or negative coverage. Coverage about gangs was used by the organization to demand city services, such as improved street lighting, heightened police presence, and recreational facilities, such as the swimming pool. These were tangible accomplishments that the community leaders could point to as evidence of an organizational strategy that worked. An important component of this successful strategy is that these leaders did not challenge the media portrayals of gangs in the neighborhood. Instead they used such inaccurate portrayals to further their goals. In contrast to this strategy, another group of neighborhood leaders refused to accept or to leave unchallenged local television news' portrayal of their neighborhood as overrun by gangs.

In an older Mexican American neighborhood, which borders the downtown area, community leaders related a different experience with television news. These leaders complained that, regardless of the number of press releases sent or phone calls made, the television stations, as well as other media, failed to cover their activities. This organization, in one of the areas of town with a reputation for having one of the worst gang problems in the city, had sponsored a Halloween party for the kids in the neighborhood. According to one leader, more than 800 kids had participated.

> But not one media showed up. The newspaper was not there. There wasn't one incident. There wasn't a fight or anything near a fight. All it was was people that came out of their homes, the kids that came and enjoyed a safe Halloween. (Personal communication)

According to this informant, on the evening of the Halloween party, the news media failed to show up because there was no fear of a drive-by shooting, no fear of gang violence, or any other kind of violence. He pointed out that "if there's a fight, the media are out here in a New York minute."

When asked if the media had been informed about the activity, he said that they had been.

> We put out press releases, as a matter of fact all last week. All last week. We always do it two weeks [before] for the [television] media [because] of the turnaround time [that they need]. (Community leader, personal communication)

A major difference between this group and the others is that this group took a perspective on the Mexican American gang problem that differed from the mainstream. This organization had members that

Community Leaders

questioned television news' presentations about gangs. Leaders of this organization also expressed doubts about police statistics on gangs. Finally, these leaders were willing to introduce the issue of race into the reporting of gangs, noting that many of the gang stories on local television news were racist portrayals of the Mexican American community.

This organization had invited the news media, including local television, to several events. When asked if they had a hard time convincing the media to cover their stories, the reply was:

> Oh, yea. Big time. Because again, it's not newsworthy to them to show a *quinceñera* on their newscast. But it is newsworthy for them to show boy scout troops in the northwest part of the city that are on a hiking trip. Little cute white boys and white girls, na, na, na, look at this. But for them to come to a *quinceñiera* in this part of town!? Again, it's cultural ignorance and the racist attitudes that they have. (Personal communication)

When asked about gangs in the neighborhood, this source said that, while he does not dispute that there may be some gangs in the neighborhood, the news media's focus on the gang problem distorts the image of the neighborhood and especially of the young people in the neighborhood. But much of this distortion, he said, was the result of Mexican Americans who are willing to play up the gang theme.

> See, I'm not going to be supported or be funded by the city, the police association, or by the Hispanic Chamber of Commerce or these types of organizations for going out and preaching good to our kids. But if I go out there and I say, "hey, I grew up in the barrio and I was a member of a gang and I'm going to go out there and speak about it," I'll become a hot item and I can be sent to all the high schools to talk about it. (Personal communication)

The media were accused of providing a forum for those willing to play up the gang theme while ignoring those who chose to focus on the more positive aspects and features of the Mexican American community.

> Again it goes back to "what do you mean by a gang?" Is that volleyball team a gang? Or is it a volleyball team? Now, this team, this group, may be identified or portrayed as a gang, and they're playing volleyball. Go to the YMCA, and it's a neighborhood group of girls that is playing volleyball. See, so you have two different types of covers, or focus, that

come out. The media will come out and do a story on girls that decided to play volleyball, and therefore are playing in an organized sport as opposed to being out there in the streets. (Personal communication)

It is clear from this leader's comments that he rejected the commonsense views about gangs in the Mexican American community. While there was a desire to get television news to cover some of his organization's activities there was also a resistance to easily produced television news stories based on what he claimed were false assumptions about the young people in the neighborhood. In his statements there is a challenge to mainstream views about Mexican American gangs and gang members. Such a challenge would make it difficult to produce a television news story about this neighborhood.

Those groups that were more successful in getting media attention made persistent efforts to contact news station departments, including individual reporters. These groups often provided events that could be videotaped by the television news team. Graffiti stings, graffiti "washouts"—neighborhood residents painting over graffiti—and other events of this type were orchestrated with the news media in mind. These events resulted in material that the stations could use in the newscast. Important also is that these events, which could be videotaped and developed into stories, did not detract from the usual gang story line, rather they reinforced it. In other words the stories were "easy" for television reporters to produce (Dorfman & Schiraldi, 2001, p. 27). These stories allowed reporters to continue to report their "gang" stories as they had before. News department producers and anchors had no problem with how the stories were framed. These types of stories did not challenge "common sense" about gangs but confirmed it.

In contrast, the groups and individuals who sought media attention but were not very successful in getting it tended to be loosely organized and deviated from the standard gang story that reporters, anchors, and producers have come to expect.

This is a significant finding, because many writers have stated that newsworthiness is directly related to opposition or deviation. That is, the more a group is different from the mainstream, the higher its chances of getting coverage—the "man bites dog" view of journalism. With the Mexican American gang story, this does not always seem to be the case. On the one hand, an argument can be made that local television news produces and airs stories about Mexican American youth gangs because this social group is in opposition to and deviates from middle-class values. On the other hand, local television news does not appear to be welcoming of any material provided by sources that may deviate from the theme of the gang as a negative social phenomenon. Sources that provide information that goes against the stereotypical perception of the Mexican American community as a gang-infested area where residents are afraid to go out at night is not material embraced by television news reporters. Indeed, it is rare to find a gang story that does not stick to the idea that gangs are a negative phenomenon that needs to be wiped out. Only one time in more than a two-year period of researching this topic did I come across a television story in which a reporter, who happened to be an African American female, used the term "good gangs" in her story. Reporting on a meeting to discuss the gang problem in Austin, the reporter ended her story by stating: "Some of the options that will be talked about tonight include combining all of the anti-gang programs here in Austin. Organizers say they want the good gangs to be better and stronger than the bad gangs" (Local television news story aired September 1, 1993, 6:00 P.M.). The use of the term "gang" in a story is strongly associated with "bad." Equally strong is the association between "gang" and minority youths. These perceptions are an extension of the association among reporters between juvenile crime and inner city and minority youth (Dorfman & Schiraldi, 2001), which is an extension of the stereotype promoted by "gang" professionals such as Sgt. Wes McBride of the Los Angeles County Sheriff's Department and author of *Understanding Street Gangs*. Other authors have also noted that the gang phenomenon is strongly associated with minority inner-city youths. Producing "positive" stories about Mexican American youths is rare. Producing positive stories about Mexican American youth gangs is nonexistent, although some researchers have pointed out that neighborhood groups can be beneficial to many teens. Group affiliation can provide a respite from family problems, school pressures, and social discrimination, especially in neighborhoods where resources for young people are scarce. Such gang issues are rarely, if ever, covered by the news media.

 The structure of an organization also seems to have an impact on how effective the organization is in attracting attention of the news media. In general, the more hierarchical an organization, the more successful it will be in getting the attention of news organizations. The community leader who invited the reporter to the graffiti sting never mentioned the members of his organization. He used the personal pronoun "I" often when discussing the organization and its involvement with television news. In contrast, the leader of the organization that organized the Halloween party used "we" when discussing his organization's plans. This organization worked by consensus and the leadership seemed less centralized. If this organization wanted to take a public stand on some issue, a majority of the members had to vote to do so. Without a consensus, no action would be taken.

When the issue of a curfew for persons under the age of seventeen was put to a vote, the organization that had set up the graffiti sting operation was in favor of it. Its leaders made appearances at several hearings held across town to discuss the issue of the curfew. The organization that had organized the Halloween party could not reach a consensus on the matter, thus, no position was officially taken. Individual members were free to talk to the news media about what they thought about the curfew, but the leadership could not make a statement to the news media on behalf of the organization.

Strong leadership, a focused message, and a narrative that does not challenge mainstream thinking appear to be prerequisites for getting media attention focused on the Mexican American youth gang news story for local television news. What the implications of this are for intelligent debate on this issue, and the effect this can have on social policy, will be discussed later.

RESOURCES

Community leaders are often associated with organization that are resource-poor. Neighborhood organizations, social service agencies, and church groups usually have considerably less resources, such as money, equipment, and personnel, than do television news organizations and police departments.

The social service agency may be funded by a government entity, such as the federal government, the state, county, or city. Other agencies may be funded by churches or other religious organizations. Still others may be funded by private foundations or philanthropic organizations. Most social service agencies, especially the larger ones, may receive assistance from several, if not all, of these sources. Church-sponsored organizations might receive funds from a variety of sources, including government organizations. These sources of funding are important to point out because it is one way that the social service organization is tied to the larger social and economic system and in this way also tied to the mainstream ideas of the economic system. As Platt (1977) has shown in his work on the social programs designed to help children and teenagers at the turn of the twentieth century, these organizations were founded by feminist reformers who tended to belong to the upper echelons of society (see Chapter 4: Maternal Justice, pp. 75–100). The leading figures of this movement tended to have husbands who were well connected to the business elite. Funding for these programs was often made possible through these connections. However, it was not only money that was made available for these programs. Along with funding came a set of middle-class values, beliefs, and way of life. These organizations then did not operate apart from the larger social structure but were themselves produced and nurtured by it. This is why it is important to understand the funding of social service organizations. While it is important not to oversimplify the relationship between donating money and imposing a cultural belief system, it is also important to keep in mind that money usually comes with strings attached.

This is one of the reasons that the social service organization's approach to the Mexican American youth gang is not likely to differ much from the approaches found in society as a whole. While social service organizations may argue for more rehabilitative than retributive approaches for dealing with the Mexican American youth gang, they will likely remain within the bounds imposed by commonsense thinking about the Mexican American youth gang. This means that, while an organization may call for spending more on education and social service programs for Mexican American youth, it will still adhere to the belief that Mexican American youths are prone to gang membership, likely to take drugs, and inclined to engage in acts of senseless violence. While its perspective on Mexican American youth gangs may vary in some ways from those of the police, the overall philosophy of the social service organization designed to help Mexican American youths stay away from gangs, drugs, and violence will reflect mainstream or "commonsense" approaches. For example, rather than call for more retributive measures against young people—such as intensified crack-downs by the police on Mexican American youths and increased prison sentences—social service agency employees and neighborhood leaders may instead call for more community programs and activities designed to give young people alternatives to those activities believed to foster criminal activity, often referred to as "life on the streets." This pattern is not new. Moore (1978), in her study of Mexican American gangs in Los Angeles, has written "Almost without pause since the early 1950s, one or another kind of program has been a regular part of the environment of the barrio gangs" (p. 42).

The reporter introduced earlier in Chapter 3 and who produced the three-part series on gangs said that one of her objectives in producing that series was to show the viewers "what it's like out on the streets" (Reporter, personal communicaiton). The prevailing idea is that anyone who grows up in a certain part of town "grew up on the streets." One source for this study complained that when he first started working with a social service program he was introduced as someone who was successful because while he had grown up on the streets, he was now an employee of the city department of parks and recreation. He resented being portrayed as someone who was from a broken home, forced to fend for himself in the "barrio."

> Came from the streets?! My grandmother raised me in a house, a home. I wasn't someone who slept out on the streets every night or even every now and then. I came from a home with a family foundation, a strong family foundation, with strong Catholic values. But yet to them I was someone that came from the streets. I'm going "Wow! That's news to me!" (Community leader, personal communication)

This is a dilemma for many Mexican American social service workers. On the one hand, they are expected to serve as role models for the youth in the community. In order to serve as role models for young people, some community leaders reinvent themselves. Rather than the middle-class backgrounds many of them experienced growing up, they relate stories about growing up poor, being in a gang, watching friends die, and then as a result of some fortuitous incident taking advantage of school and seeking an education as a way of leaving behind a life of poverty and crime. No doubt some persons in the community do have these types of experiences. However, the vast majority of persons who grew up in Mexican American neighborhoods, as we learned in earlier chapters, never joined a gang, were never arrested, and, like the community leader quoted above, grew up in a home with a nurturing family. While the funding sources for these programs may not overtly encourage this type of narrative, they certainly do not discourage it. After all, such narratives support the work of such organizations. In turn, the news media seek such stories of "life on the streets" because it is unique and dramatic and because it offers the opportunity to write a "success" story.

Often one or more of the persons who work for community organizations will be asked for comments about the gang situation by television news reporters. It is not unusual for the employees of these organizations to make themselves available for comments to the news media. While no one can be forced to appear on camera, these organizations are seeking publicity to promote their work in the community. One counselor who oversees several programs designed to help primarily young Mexican Americans explained the relationship between media coverage, especially television news, and funding by pointing out that when discussion about funding by municipal and county governments comes up, the more prominent a program the less time that needs to be spent making the persons voting on funding aware of the program. The more a program is known the more likely that it will be funded:

> We did an octane booster campaign to help the community know what octane was, and it was a rally kind of thing, and we informed [the media] that we were going to be doing that, and, so we contacted the media and they came out and filmed all of the people, the community people going and putting flyers and taking them in the community, that kind of stuff. So, anything of that nature we would go ahead and try to get the media involved. (Social Service Program Director, personal communication)

All community organizations are trying to get media attention. The staffs of these organizations write press releases, contact reporters, make themselves available for radio talk shows, and although rare, may even write opinion pieces for the local newspaper. The managers of social service agencies know that often they are competing against other social service agencies in the area for limited funds. One selling point when trying to attract the attention of television news stations is "success."

As noted earlier in this chapter, one of the favorite stories of local television news is the "success story." At times, social service organizations will initiate news coverage about persons who have managed, or are trying, to separate themselves from a Mexican American gang. At others, just as they do with the police department, newsworkers will contact the social service agency to find out if any material that can be shaped into a "success" news story is available.

> I also call several organizations who provide a lot of assistance to gang members and ask them for success stories 'cause you don't want to do a series that just goes against everything, you know, this is bad, this is horrible, it's never going to be fixed. You want to give those who are

out there who might need some help the opportunity to get the help they need. (Reporter, personal communication)

There are two primary reasons why the social service agency seeks such coverage. The first is to publicize its efforts and create an awareness about the services being provided to the community by the agency. In this sense, seeking coverage by local television news amounts to a public relations effort. The second reason, related to the first, is to facilitate the raising of funds for the organization. One supervisor of a youth leaders program said presentations are a way for her group to raise some funds. The news media helped spread the word about her organization when one of the youths, a former gang member, was profiled. As a result, she was invited by organizations around town to present a panel discussion on the gang problems in the city. At these panel discussions, she makes a pitch for support for her program but there is no set fee for the presentations. The donations that the organization receives for these presentations are used to provide pizza and soft drinks for those adolescents who come by the center.

> It [the profile on the local television station] got the word out and ... since then we've gotten some calls. So the money that I make from these conferences—some give a hundred, some give us a little money, we don't make big money here—we use for the kids, to feed them. (Social Service Coordinator, personal communication)

As funding cycles come around, social service organizations attempt to attract media attention because, as one social worker employed by an agency that provides services primarily to the Mexican American community in the eastern part of the city said, "the more people know about your program and what you are doing, the better the chances that you'll get funded." In the television market studied, there are several organizations that contribute or attempt to contribute information to the news media about the work they do with youth in general and gangs in particular. All of them were attempting to promote their agencies via the news media. Neighborhood organizations, churches, and other groups also contact the news media and provide information about the problems they may be having with gangs in the neighborhood as well as solutions that these organizations are proposing.

One organization, a neighborhood association, had a reputation with the television news reporters I interviewed. One reporter described the association as "media savvy," and when I asked him how he found out about it, he said that it is the type of organization that maintains close contact with the news media: "They let you know they're around" (TV reporter, personal communication). The president of that organization always carried a pager and made his pager number available to members of the news media. He made it known that they could call him at any time either on his pager, at home, or at work.

The pager, used extensively in the early 1990s just before the proliferation of cell phones, was a communication technology that gave community organizations the opportunity to stay in contact with the news media including television news reporters. Inexpensive pagers became a resource that neighborhood leaders could use to increase their chances of getting their voices heard on local news. The leader who called the station to invite a reporter to accompany him on a graffiti sting carried a cell phone.

These organizations, like anyone else going before television cameras, attempt to present the work that they do in the best possible light. They may provide information about the extent of the gang problem and relate it to a lack of resources in the neighborhood. This lack of resources can be anything from lack of role models or work skills to a lack of opportunities to develop physically and psychologically through organized sports or supervised social events, like dances and picnics.

Community leaders, then, present themselves and their organizations as providing the means through which the teenagers served by an agency or program can acquire the skills to overcome the problems of gangs, drugs, and violence. The question of whether gangs, drugs, and violence are a serious problem in the Mexican American community is rarely raised. The assumption is that they are.

It is important to understand that social service organizations actively seek the attention of the news media. Their goal, in light of limited budgets, is to use the media, especially television news, to raise awareness in the viewers about the services they offer and the contribution they are making to the community. At a time when social service programs were being threatened with budget cuts or elimination altogether, the news media represented a cost-effective, albeit not very dependable, method for promoting an agency or service. One program director I spoke with had recently received coverage from a local television station. The story had aired in early 1995. As a result of the coverage, she received several calls from organizations, clubs, and workshop organizers to speak about the problems of young people in the community. When asked to comment on the value of the news coverage for her program she said:

> Very important. Because like I said, every year I have to fight [to get funded]. I don't know if I'm going to be funded the next year. I am not secure here. (Social Service Program Director, personal communication)

The public relations element that is an important feature of seeking and cooperating with reporters to get television news coverage means that the production of these stories cannot be left to chance. Community and agency leaders must be selective of the topics of the news stories and the individuals who will personify the organization. By selecting certain information about a program or programs, or individuals involved with the program as clients, the agency also exerts some influence on the content of Mexican American gang stories.

In the typical television news story about a social service agency, the agency employees provide newsworkers with information and facts about the program and a brief description of the problem. Clients, usually the primary focus of the news stories—recall rule 3 from Rules for Great Storytelling: "Focus on the people affected"—serve as living examples of the appropriateness of the methods employed by the agency. The selection of information about the agency and agency employees and clients who will appear on camera must be done not only in accordance with the needs of the agency but also in accordance with the needs of the news media in order to make the production of a news story attractive to the assignments editor, reporter, and producer. Some activity that can be videotaped needs to be offered to the television news crew. Such activity must be attractive enough to lure the television news crew away from other events that may be going on at the same time. File cabinets or "in boxes" at television news stations are filled with press releases about events planned days and even weeks before they are scheduled. These press releases are organized by date. Assignments editors and reporters pull the file for the current day or the following day to examine what will be happening and select from those releases that look the most promising. Social service agencies vie for news media attention with other groups and organizations in the community.

Part of the information provided to the reporter by social service agencies is the success case or cases. The "former" gang member or current gang member who is trying to get out of a gang is presented as an example of how the lives of Mexican American teenagers can change. The person identified as a former gang member in a story that appeared on June 4, 1993, is one example. This person said that, if he had not received help from the police gang unit and a social service organization in town, he would be robbing people and creating other types of problems. Another station presented a Mexican American family in which the teenage son states that if his family had not received help he would be either dead or in jail (November 10, 1993, 6:00 P.M.).

Understandably, stories about teenagers who refuse the services or who accept the services but have no intention of leaving the gang lifestyle behind are rarely, if ever, presented to the reporter for interviews. To maintain a positive image in the community, a social service agency needs to stress its successes. Teenagers are said to have to want to change as a condition for seeing positive results, which are tacitly understood to mean staying in school, not using drugs, and dressing in a manner that does not include what became stereotypical symbols of the gang lifestyle. Such symbols include flannel shirts buttoned only at the collar, baggy pants worn below the waist, bandannas, or "colors" sticking out of back pockets, and baseball caps worn backwards.

The "gang member" chosen by the social service agency for presentation to the mass media is usually not the "average" gang member. Rather it is the individual that best exemplifies the ideals, goals, and philosophy of the agency. So, for example, the students cleaning up the yard of a senior citizen's home or the teens participating in a weight lifting program or sent to an alternative learning center are not selected by the agency or the news media at random. They are chosen because they are believed by the agency heads to best represent what the program is trying to accomplish. Often, agency clients are groomed for presentations. One organization that has its members make public presentations on behalf of that organization prepares the panelists for public appearances.

> We talk about it. We explain what is going to happen [at the public presentations], who's going to do what part, we train them, we teach them how to do presentations. We teach them leadership skills, communication skills. (Social Service Program Director, personal communication)

This control over who will represent the agency and what information to share and which to hold back gives these organizations considerable influence over the content that the television news story will relate to viewers.

Often, however, the agency, regardless of how much it wants to control the message, is unable to mold the information it is making available to the news media. One agency had cooperated with a television news reporter for a profile of one of its members. The person profiled was selected because he had been with the agency for several months and managed to win a scholarship to a prestigious state university. About one year before the profile was produced, his home had been shot at by "rival gang members." The reporter started the story by saying "Joe is hitting the books right now but a year ago he was hitting people." The person profiled in the television news feature later said: "I didn't like the beginning. When they said 'Joe is hitting the books right now but a year ago he was hitting people,' I didn't much like that at all." Joe admitted that he had been in fights in the past but only to defend himself. If someone was threatening him or one of his friends at school he would not hesitate to fight. However, he said that the introduction to the news story made it seem as if he was a violent person who had been looking for people to beat up. When asked where the reporter got the information about Joe hitting people, the director of a social service program Joe was involved with said, "All he said [to the reporter] was that he was a gang member." Joe added, "And that's all I said." I then asked, "Did they make up that piece about you hitting people?" The agency director replied by nodding her head and saying "A-ha. [That reporter] is good at that. She's very good at that. You got to watch what you say with her."

Reporters will take certain liberties with stories about Mexican American youth gangs that go far beyond the bounds of good journalism. As this example shows, some people in the community are convinced that some reporters working on stories about Mexican American youth gangs will fabricate material. This is what the agency director meant when she said that "All he said was that he was a gang member." Once that information is divulged, reporters feel that they can incorporate various assumptions into their stories.

Another example of an assumption that particularly bothered the community service director, the young man profiled, and members of his family is that at one point in the news story he was shown with his younger sister. The reporter referred to the sister as a "wanna-be." In fact, the little girl had never expressed an interest in joining a gang. The parents of these two children were said to have been infuriated with the reporter for making such a statement about their daughter.

There are other examples of parents being very uncomfortable when the news media begin to label their children as "gang members" or as children who aspire to be gang members, "wanna-be's." Being associated with a gang, being labeled a "gang member," or defined as a "wanna-be" is recognized by people in the Mexican American community as extremely harmful. However, there is little that they can do to combat such labels when powerful cultural beliefs facilitate such behavior. For example, one community leader said that many parents would not allow their children to participate in any activities, such as organized baseball games for gang members, because of the stigma that goes along with such participation. He said that many parents considered it repulsive that their children could only play baseball if willing to associate themselves in some way with gang imagery.

> I know parents who won't take their kids to the program. They say, "My kid is not a gang member. My kid, we don't even drink in my home, much less do drugs." And [I won't] have my kids participating in that program when one of the directives of that program is to listen to this (anti)gang preaching.

Again, a lack of resources with which to control one's image in the community and consequently in the news media explains much of these distortions. The example in which a gang member was portrayed as someone who was hitting people at random and his younger sister portrayed as a wanna-be can be largely explained by the fact that the family, the social service agency that arranged the interviews, and the individuals themselves all lack the resources that would allow them to craft a more positive image that could be delivered to the news media. The parents who did not want their children to participate in organized sports activities associated with "gangs" also are at a disadvantage because of their lack of access to resources. Access to persons with experience in the news media and knowledge about public relations would be beneficial for these groups and individuals. Having persons write copy that could be used in stories would likely tilt the balance of the story in the person or agency's favor. Knowing how photographers will shoot a story could give the subject of the story an advantage. The subject could arrange for certain shots and not others. Finally, legal advice could go far in assuring more fair and accurate presentation on local television news. Having an attorney present while the production of the story is taking place would send a clear message to the reporter and the station's managers that accuracy and fairness will be expected at every step of the production process or serious legal and financial consequences may be suffered by the news department and staff. In an era of intense competition between stations for advertising dollars, such a threat may be enough to keep most newsworkers from even raising the issue of gangs.

For one activist, the reporting on antigang programs was seen as a way to keep the Mexican American community from taking a leadership role in important matters. He blamed some leaders in the Mexican American community for "selling out" the young people in the community. The gang theme was seen as a red herring.

> It's a falsification of reality. It's political. If the media are buying into it, hey, they'll play to it. Here you have the media show up and they'll exploit the kids. They'll say, "all these teens these are wanna-be gang members. Had they not been in this program they'd probably be gang members right now." So the media go out and shoots and then they'll highlight the program. (Community leader, personal communication)

This person went on to say that having a "gang problem" amounted to a political ploy to distract the Mexican American community from other more pressing and more substantial issues. When leaders in the Mexican American community want to challenge the status quo or become involved in how the city is run, city leaders can tell them, "you need to be taking care of your gang problems" (Community leader, personal communication).

This small group of activists raised questions that were never heard on local television news. For example, like the police administrator in the previous chapter, one community leader interviewed raised the question of how the police and the news media come to label a drug deal or a shooting as "gang" activity.

> You know, it seems like some sort of accomplishment for [the police department] to say "Oh, it was gang related," as opposed to saying, "Well, it was a drug deal." Because again, your drug dealers, most of your drug dealers, are your sellers and not the creators of the product. So if one kid is selling drugs is he a gang member or is he a drug seller? There's a difference . . . I don't see Latin Kings going by, it may be some person that went and happened to know that this person was there at a party, an individual, but its tied to the Latin Kings. For example, I might go to the bank and rob a bank as an individual. "Oh, he's with [that community group]. It's the community group that went and robbed the bank." The community group had nothing to do with it. I was act-

ing on my own as an individual. But see we don't get that kind of a possibility. It's got to be "gang related."

This community leader went on to also criticize reporters who attempt to cover the gang issue for local television news.

> I guess the most fun with the media that I've had is with your socially conscious, supposedly liberal Anglo reporters. If I play the "I'm a gang member" role they get all excited like "I'm really talking to a gang member."

Mexican American reporters he found to be patronizing:

> They come in and they exploit us to the extreme. Like, "because I'm a Mexican reporter or a Hispanic reporter, I can get more out of you than an Anglo reporter could. Therefore I'm one of you." My response is, "there's nothing to say. What is there to say? What is there that I'm supposed to tell you?"

This organization's approach to the gang problem was too far removed from the mainstream to make any sense to the television audience. There was a gang problem that this organization felt needed to be addressed, but it wasn't the gang problem the community was concerned with at the time:

> You want to talk about gangs? To me the city council is a gang. The chamber of commerce is a gang, coming into our area and taking over and in a sense controlling. Controlling our people and wanting to limit our ability economically and politically—that's a gang. Now, why don't we address that gang problem? (Community leader, personal communication)

It is not difficult to see why this group of activists was overlooked by television news when stories about gangs were produced. Members of this organization had histories as activists going back to the early 1960s. While they would like to comment on the gang situation, they are considered passé, rabble-rousers, or unreasonable. One reporter, commenting on the membership of this organization that had complained about the unfair treatment of Latinos including stories about gangs on local television news, said that their approach was to "just bitch about things." She went on to say that instead of dealing with the problem rationally they resort to name-calling using terms like "racist, racial bias, and bigots, instead of dealing with it in an educated way, like the Chamber [Hispanic Chamber of Commerce] wanted to do." In this example, there is evidence of how the perceptions of the reporter can influence the selection of persons who appear in news stories about Mexican American youth gangs.

This examination of the influence of community leaders on the Mexican American youth gang story shows that not all community leaders enjoy equal access to the news media. Some leaders are clearly favored by television news reporters. Those leaders who are willing to adapt to mainstream notions of what gangs and gang members are like as well as accept the commonsense approaches for dealing with the "problem" of youth gangs stand a better chance of getting their agency profiled on local television news.

Another set of community leaders who challenge mainstream notions about gangs and gang members, and who are willing to politicize the gang problem, tend to be overlooked by television news reporters. Their view of the problem of gangs does not fit easily into the production process. Thus, their message is often left out of the local television news program.

Chapter 6
Conclusion

The Mexican American youth gang as it appears on local television news is a myth. From the use of the word "gang" and how it is applied by newsworkers almost exclusively to inner city minority youths, to the concern about Mexican American youths taking over entire areas of the city, local television news has demonstrated a lack of professionalism and fair reporting.

There is no doubt that some Mexican American gangs do exist, but these are very small in number. Also, membership in these gangs is small and rather stable over long periods of time. Reports about a growing gang problem and increasingly violent gang members speak more to the fears of suburban middle-class citizens, about the growing number of minority youth in large metropolitan centers, than to any documented evidence about qualitative changes in inner-city minority youths.

Most activity that is referred to as "gang related" on local television news is often an assumption on the part of reporters or the police. Often what is said to be a "gang-related" crime is in fact the work of an individual or individuals who are acting on their own and not as members of some organized effort.

Many television journalists claim that when they are producing stories about Mexican American youth gangs they are simply holding up a mirror to society. They tend to point to the professional ideal of objectivity in the news as a way of diffusing criticism of their reports. However, several researchers have found that news production is not objective in the sense that the reporter and the rest of the news team cannot be separate and apart from the events they cover as well as a the stories they produce. Through historical forces, education, and routines of producing stories, journalists are closely tied to the events they cover.

Still another argument used by reporters is that they are merely conveying the information provided to them by their sources. Yet we have seen how the collection and distribution of information is related to access to resources. Those groups and organizations with access to resources have a distinct advantage in getting their version of events before the pubic via the mass media. Sources sensitive to the needs of television news reporters can package information in a way that will improve its chances of making it on the air with minimum modification.

In this book, I have traced the routines of television news production and found patterns of distortion about the Mexican American youth gang in local television news stories. These distortions have their roots in the ethnic conflicts of the early 1800s. Ethnic tensions resulting from competition for control over economic and natural resources, such as trade routes, cattle, and land, promoted one-dimensional views of Mexicans. Military conflicts, including wars between the United States and Mexico, further solidified stereotypical ideas held by whites about Mexicans.

Popular culture in the mid to late 1800s and early 1900s, expressed in the form of pulp fiction and advertiser-based newspapers, provided a forum for the expression of those fears and apprehensions many white readers felt about the Mexican population. As times changed the forms of expression of those fears and apprehensions also changed.

Segregation between Mexicans and whites in the Southwest was a manifestation of the fears whites held about the dangers of mixing with an "inferior" people. With the removal of legal and social barriers that kept the two groups apart, new fears and concerns, still grounded in the past, developed. Newsreels about the Mexican revolution in the 1910s and newspaper stories in the 1930s about the zoot-suit riots and the *pachuco* gangs reported to be responsible for them, played on the white, middle-class fears of a growing Mexican population within

U.S. borders. News stories about inner-city youth gangs are but the latest manifestation of those fears.

As a profit-driven mass medium, local television news' role is not to challenge the status quo so much as to reinforce the social, economic, and political order. One of the key points of this book has been that local television news is not an objective report of the events of the day. Instead, it is an interpretation of selected events for the purpose of earning profits and maintaining the consensus that makes possible the hegemonic order. News stories are more akin to morality tales than to objective reports.

On any given day, the stories that make up the local newscast are a fraction of the possible stories that could be reported as "news." Rather than a series of random events, news stories are selected and in this way the newscast is constructed. In a profit-driven environment, the newscast is designed to attract the largest possible audience in order to achieve the highest possible earnings. Broadcast journalism as practiced in the United States and many other countries today is not so much profit driven as it is "maximum profit-driven" journalism.

The key to attracting the largest possible audience is to reinforce, not challenge, the prevailing ideas about the world. The moral of news stories is that the values, beliefs, and ideas of the largest and wealthiest audience members are the only values, beliefs, and ideas that matter. The labeling of Mexican American youths as "gang members," or certain neighborhoods as "gang infested," and the development of strategies to deal with the gang problem, such as neighborhood sweeps, boot camps, antigang programs, juvenile detention centers, and prisons, are the result of white middle-class values and beliefs about minority inner-city youths and ideas about what the world should be like. Local television news reinforces the ideas of white, suburban, middle-class viewers in order to attract this large audience, which is then sold to advertisers.

Reporters, through the routines of news production, interact with persons and institutions that reinforce the prevailing values, beliefs, and ideas. As they go about their work of collecting information and constructing stories about Mexican American youth gangs for the newscasts, television journalists inadvertently favor those groups and organizations with the most resources. Resources, such as people, money, and technology, can be used to promote a point of view that reinforces the prevailing social order.

One of those organizations that is relatively resource-rich is the police department. By organizing personnel, information, and technology, the police department can provide material to reporters that can be shaped into a news story with little difficulty. Largely because of the sources for these stories, namely the police, they tend to convey a "criminal justice" view of the Mexican American youth gang.

In addition to their routines and work with the police department, reporters also get information from sources other than the police. These tend to be social service organizations and community leaders. But a relative lack of resources on the part of these groups puts them at a distinct disadvantage when attempting to get their message across to viewers via local television news. The lack of money with which to collect information, hire personnel with expertise about the news media, and acquire technology that facilitates the distribution of information places these organizations at a distinct disadvantage. The more work a reporter has to do, the less likely that the organization will control the message that goes out to viewers. Those community leaders who are willing to play up the theme about a gang problem and help create a "good story" that does not challenge mainstream values and beliefs have a better chance of getting on the air. Those community leaders who refuse to play up the gang theme and instead challenge prevailing notions about gangs tend to be left out of the local television news picture.

The view of local television news stories about Mexican American youth gangs as objective reports cannot be supported. Those organizations with the resources to package information for the television news reporter on a regular basis will benefit from more favorable coverage in the long run. While there may be the occasional negative news story, such organizations will, over the long-term, receive favorable coverage. A resource-poor organization that is not able to provide a steady flow of information in a format that can easily be turned into a news story will have less control over the information it makes available to the news media. In fact, as the interviews with some community leaders made clear, information provided by resource-poor organizations to the television news reporter may be used to reinforce, rather than challenge, stereotypical notions about Mexican American youth gangs.

One important finding in this study is that news is to a large extent controlled by the prevailing ideas, beliefs, and values of the society in which it is produced. The selection of crime stories for the newscast is not natural or in any way predestined by objective reporting. Rather, crime stories fill the need on the part of maximum profit-driven journalism for producing stories at minimum cost that can attract a large audience. Such stories also reinforce the cultural values that serve as the "social glue" that holds society together.

Such stories show minority inner-city youths as violating society's norms, which are upheld by the white, suburban middle class. These norms make the current structure of society, with the white middle class receiving the most benefits, possible. To threaten such norms is to threaten the structure of social relations. Part of what it means to have power in any society is the ability to label others as "deviants." As Erikson (1966) has shown, deviance is not a quality inherent in any one individual but rather the result of the powerful and influential in society to define behavior as abnormal. The Mexican American youth gang has been defined as "abnormal" by the police and legal system, some social service providers, and the news media.

The focus now should be on how to change this situation. How can television news reporters be trained in new ways of reporting so that the myth about Mexican American youth gangs can be eliminated from television screens?

First, the myth of the Mexican American youth gang has a long history. Changing it will require some time. Introducing the history of these stereotypes in journalism classes and workshops for working broadcast journalists is the first step in reducing the number of Mexican American youth gang news stories. While stories about crime in Mexican American neighborhoods will no doubt occur and be reported, using the gang label when no hard evidence for such an assertion is available should be reduced.

Second, steps need to be taken to educate journalists about how these myths are reproduced through reporting practices. Again, through journalism classes and workshops and conferences, journalists can be shown how their style of news production tends to reinforce, rather than negate, stereotypical ideas about Mexican American youths. Television news reporters need to be encouraged and rewarded for going outside routine practices to find information and include it in stories about Mexican American youth gangs.

Third, viewers need to organize to monitor newscasts and complain to station managers and advertisers if positive responses are not forthcoming. Citizen's groups can successfully lobby for changes in how the news is produced. Relatively recent changes with respect to the identification of rape survivors, the use of ethnicity in describing suspects in crimes, and the inclusion of persons of color as expert sources for a variety of topics are three of the most noteworthy. Television news stations do take complaints seriously if those complaints are from organized groups with a well-focused strategy. Finally, if complaints fall on deaf ears, using the legal system to sue reporters and television stations when false information about Mexican American youths and Mexican American neighborhoods is disseminated should remain an option. The proceeds from successful lawsuits could be used to establish learning centers, sports complexes, scholarships to study broadcast journalism, and other services that benefit the community, especially the young people in the community.

News is a social process and as such it is a reflection of the social, economic, and political systems that dominate a community. This is why the Mexican American youth gang news story can change over time and eventually fade away. The key to such change is having the will and developing a strategy for elimination of the Mexican American youth gang story on local television news.

Bibliography

Acland, C. (1995). *Youth, Murder, Spectacle: The Cultural Politics of Youth in Crisis*. San Francisco: Westview Press.
Allan, S. (1999). *News Culture*. Philadelphia: Open University Press.
Altheide, D.L. (1976). *Creating Reality: How TV News Distorts Events*. Beverly Hills: Sage.
Althusser, L. (1971). *Lenin and Philosophy and Other Essays*. New York: Monthly Review Press.
Altschull, J.H. (1995). *Agents of Power: The Media and Public Policy* (2nd ed.). White Plains, NY: Longman.
Alvord, V. (2000). "Law Challenged by 'Good Boys' Facing 16 Years." *USA Today*, September 15, p. 4A.
Ariés, P. (1962). *Centuries of Childhood: A Social History of Family Life*. New York: Vintage Books.
The Associated Press Broadcast News Handbook: Incorporating the AP Libel Manual. Compiled and edited by James R. Hood and Brad Kalbfeld. New York: Associated Press, 1982.
Ausbury, H. (1970). *The Gangs of New York: An Informal History of the Underworld*. New York: Capricorn Books.
Avril, T. (1993). "3 Chicago Police Officers Work on Unusual Beat." *Los Angeles Times*, Advance Desk, column 1, p. 22A.

Banta, B. (1990). "Teen Gets 4-year Term in Bus Stop Shootings." *Austin American-Statesman* (Dec. 21): p. B1.

Barker, G.C. (1974, c. 1950). *Pachuco: An American-Spanish Argot and Its Social Functions in Tucson, Arizona*. Tucson: University of Arizona Press.

Becker, H. (1963). *The Outsiders: Studies in the Sociology of Deviance.* London: Collier-Macmillan.

Becker, S. (1967). "Whose Side Are We On?" *Social Problems* 14(3): 239–247.

Bennett, W.J., DiIulio, J.J., & Walters, J.P. (1996). *Body Count: Moral Poverty... and How to Win America's War Against Crime and Drugs.* New York: Simon and Schuster.

Bogardus, E.S. (1926). *The City Boy and His Problems.* Los Angeles: Rotary Club of Los Angeles.

Bogardus, E. (1943). "Gangs of Mexican-American Youth." *Sociology and Social Research*, 23 (Sept./Oct.): 55–56.

Bonnie, R.J., & Whitebread, C.H. (1974). *The Marihuana Conviction: A History of Marihuana Prohibition in the United States.* Charlottesville: University Press of Virginia.

Bourdieu, P. (1986). "Forms of Capital." In J.G. Richardson (Ed.), *Handbook of Theory and Research for the Sociology of Education.* Pp. 214–258. Westport, CT: Greenwood.

Breed, W. (1955). "Social Control in the Newsroom: A Functional Analysis." *Social Forces* 33 (May 1955): 326–35.

Brooks, B.S., Kennedy, G., Moen, D.R., & Ranly, D. (1999). *News Reporting and Writing.* New York: Bedford/St. Martins.

Buhmann, E.T. (1992). *The 1992 Texas Attorney General's Gang Report.* Austin: Office of the Attorney General, Research & Policy Management Division.

Bullington, B. (1977). *Heroin Use in the Barrio.* Lexington, MA: D.C. Heath.

Carey, J.W. (1992). *Communication as Culture: Essays on Media and Society.* Boston: Union Hyman.

Center for Integration and Improvement of Journalism. (1994). *News Watch: A Critical Look at Coverage of People of Color.* A Unity-94 Project. San Francisco: San Francisco State University.

Chibnall, S. (1977). *Law and Order News: An Analysis of Crime Reporting in the British Press.* London: Tavistock Publications.

Clendenen, C.C. (1972). *The United States and Pancho Villa: A Study in Unconventional Diplomacy.* Port Washington, NY: Kennikat Press.

Cohen, A. (1955). *Delinquent Boys: The Culture of the Gang.* Illinois: Free Press.

Cohen, S. (1972). *Folk Devils and Moral Panics: The Creation of the Mods and Rockers.* London: MacGibbon & Kee.

Cortés, C.E. (January, 1993). "Power, Passivity and Pluralism: Mass Media in the Development of Latino Culture and Identity." *Latino Studies Journal* 4(1): 3–22.
Dahlgren, P., & Sparks, C. (1996). *Journalism and Popular Culture*. Thousand Oaks: Sage.
De Fleur, M.L. and Ball-Rockeach, S. (1989). *Theories of Mass Communication*. (5th ed.). White Plains: Longman.
Diamond, E. (1975). *The Tin Kazoo: Politics, Television, and the News*. Cambridge, MA: MIT Press.
Domer, M. (1955). *The Zoot-Suit Riot: A Culmination of Social Tensions in Los Angeles*. Unpublished master's thesis, Claremont Graduate School, Claremont, California.
Dorfman, L., & Schiraldi, V. (April 2001). *Youth, Race and Crime in the News*. Berkeley: Media Studies Group.
Duffus, R.L. (1930). *The Santa Fe Trail*. New York: Longman, Green.
Durkheim, E. (1965). *The Elementary Forms of Religious Life*. New York: Free Press.
Elliott, P. (1972). *The Making of a Television Series*. London: Constable.
Emery, M., Emery, E., and Roberts, N.L. (1996). *The Press in America: An Interpretative History of the Mass Media*. Needham Heights, MA: Allyn and Bacon.
Entman, R.M. (1992). "Blacks in the News: Television, Modern Racism and Cultural Change." *Journalism Quarterly*, 69(Summer): 341–361.
Ericksen, C.A. (1981). "Hispanic Americans and the Press." *Journal of Intergroup Relations* 9(1): 3–17.
Ericson, R.V., Baranek, P.M., & Chan, J.B.L. (1989). *Negotiating Control: A Study of News Sources*. Toronto: University of Toronto Press.
Erikson, K.T. (1966). *Wayward Puritans: A Study in the Sociology of Deviance*. New York: John Wiley and Sons, Inc.
Falchikov, N. (1986). "Images of Adolescence: An Investigation into the Accuracy of the Image of Adolescence by British Newspapers." *Journal of Adolescence*, 9(June): 167–180.
Femia, J.V. (1981). *Gramsci's Political Thought*. Oxford: Oxford University Press.
Ferrell, J. (1993). *Crimes of Style: Urban Graffiti and the Politics of Criminality*. New York: Garland.
Ferrell, J. & Websdale, N. (Eds.) (1999). *Making Trouble: Cultural Constructions of Crime, Deviance, and Control*. New York: Aldine de Gruyter.
Ferrell, J. & Websdale, N. (Eds.) (1996). *Making Trouble: Cutlural Constructions of Crime, Deviance and Control*. New York: Aldine de Gruyter.
Fishman, M. (1980). *Manufacturing the News*. Austin: University of Texas.
Fiske, J. (1989). *Reading the Popular*. New York: Routledge.

Fiske, J. (1996). "Popularity and the Politics of Information." In P. Dahlgren & C. Sparks (Eds.), *Journalism and Popular Culture*. Thousand Oaks: Sage.

Fiske, J., & Hartley, J. (1978). *Reading Television*. London: Routledge.

Gandy, O. (1982). *Beyond Agenda Setting*. Norwood, NJ: Ablex Publishing Co.

Gans, H.J. (1980). *Deciding What's News*. New York: Vintage Books.

Gerbner, G., Gross, L., Morgan, M., & Signorielli, N. (1994). "Growing Up with Television: The Cultivation Perspective." In J. Bryant and D. Zillmann (Eds.), *Media Effects: Advances in Theory and Research*. Pp. 17–42. Hillsdale, NJ: Lawrence Erlbaum.

Gieber, W., & Johnson, W. (1961). "The City Hall Beat." *Journalism Quarterly* 38: 289–297.

Gitlin, T. (1980). *The Whole World Is Watching: Mass Media in the Making and Unmaking of the New Left*. Berkeley: University of California Press.

Goldenberg, E.N. (1975). *Making the Papers: Access of Resource-Poor Groups to the Metropolitan Press*. Lexington, MA: D.C. Heath and Co.

Gómez-Quiñones, J. (1990). *Chicano Politics: Reality and Promise, 1940–1990*. Albuquerque: University of New Mexico Press.

Gonzales, A. (1981). *Mexicano/Chicano Gangs in Los Angeles: A Sociohistorical Case Study*. Unpublished dissertation, University of California, Berkeley, School of Social Welfare.

Gramsci, A. (1971). *Selections from the Prison Notebooks*. New York: International Publishers.

Gregg, J. (1966). *Commerce of the Prairies: Or the Journal of a Sante Fé Trader, Vol. 1*. New York: Henry G. Langley.

Habermas, J. (1991). *The Structural Transformation of the Public Sphere*. Cambridge: MIT Press.

Hagedorn, J.M. (1998). *People and Folks: Gangs, Crime and the Underclass in a Rustbelt City* (2nd ed). Chicago: Lake View Press.

Haglund, K. (1991). "Reclaiming the Community." *Austin American-Statesman*, May 8, Section A, p. A1.

Hall, S. & Jefferson, T. (Eds.). (1975). *Resistance Through Rituals: Youth Subcultures in Post-War Britain*. London: Routledge.

Hall, S., Critcher, C., Jefferson, T., Clarke, J., & Roberts, B. (1978). *Policing the Crisis: Mugging, the State, and Law and Order*. Houndmills, UK: Macmillan.

Hallin, D.C. (1986). "We Keep America on Top of the World." In T. Gitlin (Ed.), *Watching Television*. Pp. 9–41. New York: Pantheon.

Hallin, D.C. (1994). *We Keep America on Top of the World: Television Journalism and the Public Sphere*. New York: Routledge.

Hartman, P., & Husband, C. (1974). *Racism and the Mass Media*. London: Davis-Poynter.

Hebdige, D. (1979). *Subculture: The Meaning of Style*. London: Methuen.
Heider, D. (2000). *White News: Why Local News Programs Don't Cover People of Color*. Mahwah, NJ: Lawrence Erlbaum.
Heller, C.S. (1966). *Mexican American Youth: Forgotten Youth at the Crossroads*. New York: Random House.
Herman, E., & Chomsky, N. (1988). *Manufacturing Consent: The Political Economy of the Mass Media*. New York: Pantheon.
Higginbotham, S. (1990). "Cooke Moves Police to Congress Ave." *The Daily Texan*, September 21, p. 1.
Higginbotham, S. (1990). "Shooting Suspect Surrenders to APD." *The Daily Texan*, October 1, p. 1.
Himmelstein, J. (1983). *The Strange Career of Marijuana*. Westport, CT: Greenwood Press.
Holton, K. (1942). "Delinquency in War Time." *Crime Prevention Digest*, 1(12) (November).
Horkheimer, M., & Adorno, T. (1994). *Dialectic of Enlightenment*. New York: Herder and Herder.
Humphrey, N.D. (1945). "The Stereotype and the Social Types of Mexican American Youths." *The Journal of Social Psychology* 22: 69–78.
Iscoe, L.K. (1990). *Texas Teens: The Status of Adolescents*. Commission on the Mental Health of Adolescents and Young Adults. Hogg Foundation for Mental Health. Austin: University of Texas.
Jankowski, M.S. (1991). *Islands in the Street: Gangs and American Urban Society*. Los Angeles: University of California Press.
Juergens, G. (1966). *Joseph Pulitzer and the New York World*. Princeton, NJ: Princeton University Press.
Kaniss, P. (1991). *Making Local News*. Chicago: University of Chicago Press.
Kellner, D. (1990). *Television and the Crisis of Democracy*. Boulder: Westview Press.
Kerner, Otto. (1968). *Report of the National Advisory Commission on Civil Disorder*. Washington, D.C.: United States Government Printing Office.
Kitsuse, J.I., & Cicourel, A.V. (1963). "A Note on the Uses of Official Statistics." *Social Problems* 11(2) (Fall): 131–139.
Klein, M.W. (1971). *Street Gangs and Street Workers*. Englewood Cliffs, NJ: Prentice-Hall.
Kooistra, P. & Mahoney, J.S. (1999). "The Historical Roots of Tabloid TV Crime." In J. Ferrell and N. Websdale (Eds.), *Making Trouble: Cultural Constructions of Crime, Deviance, and Control*. Pp. 42–71. New York: Adline De Gruyter.
Macias, Y.R. (1971). "The Chicano Movement." In W. Moquin, C. Van Doren, & F. Rivera (Eds.), *A Documentary History of the Mexican Americans*. Pp. 499–506. New York: Bantam.
Males, M.A. (1999). *Framing Youth: Ten Myths About the Next Generation*. Monroe, ME: Common Courage.

Marcuse, H. (1964). *One-Dimensional Man*. Boston: Beacon Press.
Martinez, D.R. (1978). "Hispanic Youth in the Barrio." *Agenda* 8(5) (January/February): 7–8.
Mauer, M. (1999). *Race to Incarcerate*. New York: The New Press.
Mazón, M. (1984). *The Zoot-Suit Riots*. Austin: University of Texas Press.
McDermott, T. (2000). "Rafael Perez: The Road to Rampart." *Los Angeles Times* (December 31), Home Edition, Part A, Part 1, p. 1, Metro Desk.
McLemore, D.S., & Romo, R. (1985). "The Origins and Development of the Mexican American People." In R.O. de la Garza, F.D. Bean, C.M. Bonjean, R. Romo, & R. Alvarez (Eds.), *The Mexican American Experience: An Interdisciplinary Anthology*. Pp. 1–32. Austin: University of Texas Press.
McManus, J.H. (1994). *Market-Driven Journalism: Let the Citizen Beware?* Thousand Oaks: Sage.
McWilliams, C. (1990). *North from Mexico: The Spanish-Speaking People of the United States*. Westport, CT: Greenwood Press.
Meier, M.S. & Rivera, F. (1972). *The Chicanos: A History of Mexican Americans*. New York: Hill and Wang.
Miller, W. (1975). *Violence by Youth Gangs and Youth Groups as a Crime Problem in Major American Cities*. Washington, DC: U.S. Department of Justice.
Montejano, D. (1987). *Anglos and Mexicans in the Making of Texas, 1836–1986*. Austin: University of Texas Press.
Moore, J.W. (1978). *Homeboys: Gangs, Drugs, and Prison in the Barrios of Los Angeles*. Philadelphia: Temple University Press.
Moore, J.W. (1991). *Going Down to the Barrio*. Philadelphia: Temple University Press.
Moore, J.W., & Vigil, J. D. (1989). "Chicano Gangs: Group Norms and Individual Factors Related to Adult Criminality." *Aztlan* 18(2): 27–44.
Moquin, W., Van Doren, C., & Rivera, F. (Eds.). (1971). *A Documentary History of the Mexican Americans*. New York: Praeger.
Morales, A. (1982). "The Mexican American Gang Member: Evaluation and Treatment." In R.M. Becerra, M. Karno, & J.I. Escobar (Eds.), *Mental Health and Hispanic Americans*. Pp. 134–155. New York: Grune and Stratton.
Morgan, P. (1990). "The Making of a Public Problem: Mexican Labor in California and the Marijuana Law of 1937." In R. Glick & J. Moore (Eds.), *Drugs in Hispanic Communities*. Pp. 233–252. New Brunswick: Rutgers University Press.
Mott, F.L. (1962). *American Journalism: A History 1690–1960*. New York: Macmillan.
Muñoz, C. (1989). *Youth Identity and Power: The Chicano Movement*. New York: Verso.

Newkirk, P. T. (2000). "Doors Are Open but Minds Are Closed." *Washington Post*, September 24, Outlook section, p. B3.

Newswatch: A Critical Look at Coverage of People of Color. (1994). A Unity '94 Project. Center for Integration and Improvement of Journalism. San Francisco State University.

Paredes, A. (1973, c. 1958). *With His Pistol in His Hand.* Austin: University of Texas Press.

Paz, O. (1961). *The Labyrinth of Solitude: Life and Thought in Mexico.* New York: Grove Press.

Pearson, G. (1983). *Hooligan: A History of Respectable Fears.* London: Macmillan Press.

Pettit, A.G. (1980). *Images of the Mexican American in Fiction and Film.* College Station: Texas A&M Press.

Platt, A.M. (1977). *The Child Savers.* Chicago: University of Chicago Press.

Potter, D.M. (1954). *People of Plenty.* Chicago: University of Chicago Press.

Quintero, F. (Summer 1998). *Diversity 2010: ASNE Goal Setback and Other Changes for Journalists of Color.* Pp. 5–19. San Francisco: News Watch Project.

Romo, H.D., & Falbo, T. (1996). *Latino High School Graduation: Defying the Odds.* Austin: University of Texas Press.

Romo, R. (1983). *East Los Angeles: History of a Barrio.* Austin: University of Texas Press.

Sánchez, G.I. (1943). "Pachucos in the Making." *Common Ground* 4(1) (Autumn):13–20.

Sanders, C.R. & Lyon, E. (1995). "Repetitive Retribution: Media Images and the Cultural Construction of Criminal Justice." In J. Ferrell and C. R. Sanders (Eds.), *Cultural Criminology.* Pp. 25–44. Boston: Northeastern University Press.

Santos, J.P. (1997). "(Re)imagining America." In E.E. Dennis and E.C. Pease (Eds.), *The Media in Black and White.* New Brunswick, NJ and London: Transaction.

Schlesinger, P., & Tumber, H. (1994). *Reporting Crime: The Media Politics of Criminal Justice.* Oxford: Clarendon Press.

Schudson, M. (1978). *Discovering the News: A Social History of American Newspapers.* New York: Basic Books.

Schudson, M. (1995). *The Power of News.* Cambridge: Harvard University Press.

Schultz, S.K. (1973). *The Culture Factory: Boston Public Schools, 1789–1860.* New York: Oxford University Press.

Serrin, W. (Ed.). (2000). *The Business of Journalism.* New York: The New Press.

Shaw, C.R. and McKay, H.D. (1969, c. 1942). *Juvenile Delinquency and Urban Areas.* Chicago: University of Chicago Press.

Shoemaker, D.J. (1984). *Theories of Delinquency: An Examination of Explanations of Delinquent Behavior.* New York: Oxford University Press.

Shoemaker, P.J. and Reese, S.D. (1991). *Mediating the Message: Theories of Influence on Mass Media Content.* White Plains, NY: Longman.

Sigal, L. (1973). "Sources Make the News." In R.K. Manoff & M. Schudson (Eds.), *Reading the News.* Pp. 9–37. New York: Pantheon.

Staten, C.M., & Hall, G.E. (Eds.). (1993). *Annual Metro City and County Data Book.* Lanham, MD: Berman Press.

Stephens, M. (1993). *Broadcast News.* 3rd ed. Fort Worth: Harcourt Brace Jovanovich.

Sum, A.M., & Fogg, W.N. (1991). "The Adolescent Poor and the Early Transition to Early Adulthood." In P.B. Edelman & J. Ladner (Eds.), *Adolescence and Poverty: Challenge for the 1990s.* Pp. 37–109. Washington, D.C.: Center for National Policy Press.

Sutherland, E.H. and Cressey, D.R. (1978). *Criminology.* 10th ed. New York: Lippincott.

Terry, D. (1992). "With Rap, Not Force, 3 Chicago Police Officers Make Progress." *New York Times,* December 5, National Desk, section 1, column 1, p. 7.

Thrasher, F.M. (1942, c. 1927). *The Gang: A Study of 1,313 Gangs in Chicago.* Chicago: University of Chicago Press.

Tuchman, G. (1978). *Making News: A Study of the Cnstruction of Reality.* New York: The Free Press.

Turner, R., & Surace, S.J. (1956). "Zoot-Suiters and Mexicans: Symbols in Crowd Behavior." *American Journal of Sociology* 62:14–20.

Turow, J. (1984). *Media Industries: The Production of News and Entertainment.* New York: Longman.

"29 Fraternities Are Subpoenaed in Hazing Inquiry." (1990). *New York Times National Sunday,* November 18, p. 26L.

U.S. Commission on Civil Rights. (1979). *Window Dressing on the Set: An Update.* Washington, DC: U.S. Government Printing Office.

U.S. Commission on Civil Rights. (1977). *Window Dressing on the Set: Women and Minorities in Television.* Washington, DC: U.S. Government Printing Office.

United States Department of Commerce. (1990). *1990 Census of the Population, General Population Characteristics, Texas, Race and Hispanic Origin.* (Table 151, p. 705). Washington, D.C.: Government Printing Office.

van Dijk, T.A. (1987). *Communicating Racism: Ethnic Prejudice in Thought and Talk.* Newbury Park, NJ: Sage.

van Dijk, T.A. (1991). *Racism and the Press.* London: Routledge.

van Dijk, T.A. (1993). "Principles of Critical Discourse Analysis." *Discourse and Society* 4 (2): 249–283.

Vargas, L. (2000). "Genderizing Latino News." *Critical Studies in Media Communication* 17: 261–293.

Vigil, J.D. (1988). *Barrio Gangs.* Austin: University of Texas Press.

Warr, M. (1994). "Public Perceptions and Reactions to Violent Offending and Victimization." In A.J. Reiss & J.A. Roth (Eds.), *Understanding and Preventing Violence*, vol. 4, Pp. 3–66. Washington, DC: National Academy Press.

Warshaw, R. (1989). "Inside the Bonds of Fraternity." *Nation 249* (6) (August 21/28): 206–209.

Weich, R.H. and Angulo, C.T. (2000). *Justice on Trial*. Washington, D.C.: Leadership Conference on Civil Rights/Leadership Conference Education Fund.

White, D. (1949). "The Gate-Keeper: A Case Study in the Selection of News." *Journalism Quarterly* 27: 383–390.

White, J. (2001). "In Northern Va. Drug Ring, Good Kids Went Bad." *Washington Post*, August 12, p. A1.

Williams, V. (2000). "Black and White and Red All Over: The Ongoing Struggle to Integrate America's Newsrooms." In W. Serrin (Ed.), *The Business of Journalism: Ten Leading Reporters and Editors on the Perils and Pitfalls of the Press*. Pp. 95–116. New York: The New Press.

Wilson, C.C., & Gutiérrez, F. (1995). *Race, Multiculturalism, and the Media*. Newbury Park, NJ: Sage.

Wilson, J.Q. (1995). "Crime and Public Policy." In J.Q. Wilson and J. Petersilia (Eds.), *Crime*. Pp. 489–507. San Francisco: Institute for Contemporary Studies Press.

Woll, A.L. (1977). *The Latin Image in American Film*. Los Angeles: UCLA Latin American Center Publications.

Woll, A.L. (1980). "Bandits and Lovers: Hispanic Images in American Film." In R. Miller (Ed.), *The Kaleidoscopic Lens: How Hollywood Views Ethnic Groups*. Pp. 54–73. Englewood Cliffs, NJ: Jerome S. Ozer.

Wright, K.N. (1985). *The Great American Crime Myth*. Westport, CT: Greenwood Press.

Zatz, M.S. (1987). "Chicano Youth Gangs and Crime: The Creation of a Moral Panic." *Contemporary Crises* 11(2):129–159.

Index

Acland, Charles R., 4
Addams, Jane, Child Saver Movement, 44, 151
Allan, Stuart, 76, 77, 103
Altheide, David L., 76, 112
Altschull, J. Herbert, 76
Anslinger, Harry J., Federal Bureau of Narcotics, 50

Beat system, 86, 87
Bennett, William, 68
Bogardus, Emory, 17, 31, 32, 44, 46, 47, 54, 55

Carey, James, 4
"Cart Wars" (Texas), 39–40
Chibnall, Steve, 86, 103
Chicano, definition of, 23
Columbine High School shooting, 10

Community leaders, 6; defined, 136–139. *See also* Chapter 5
Conquest fiction, and Mexican American stereotypes, 41
Cortez, Gregorio, and Cortez "gang," 41, 42
Critical theory, 11, 12, 21

Day, Benjamin, 35. *See also* Penny papers
Diversity (in newsrooms), 63
Drugs, and Mexican American community, 49–50, 56

Eugenics, and juvenile delinquency, 47

Femia, Joseph V., 14, 15
Finger, Henry J., and drug legislation, 50

Fraternities, college, 11, 115

Gangs: characteristics of, 6; "emerging" gang problem, 2; Mexican American youth gangs and drugs, 34; and news media, 18–21; organized baseball games, 99–101; selective use of term, 10; statistics, 74; as support group, 6
Gatekeeper theory, 62, 63
Graffiti, and local television news, 142
Gramsci, Antonio, 12; common sense, 15; hegemony, 13; historical determinism, 16; and mass media, 13, 14; and study of history, 33

"Happy news," 112
Hierarchy of credibility, 110

Liberal–pluralist perspective of news, 63, 77–78
Lombroso, Cesare, 43, 45

Manifest Destiny, 35, 37
Marijuana Tax Act, 1937, 49–50
Market-driven journalism, 113
Marketplace of ideas, 140
Media representation, 7, 8; and Battle of the Alamo, 16; in film, 32, 42–43; and Mexican stereotypes, 16; and Mexican War, 35; in popular culture, 17
Mexican Revolution and film, 43; and Mexican stereotypes, 42–44
Moore, Joan W., 6; and myths about gangs, 79–80, 130; and news media, 110; and social service programs, 151

Nativism, 32, 45
News: power, 12; professional values in, 84–86; as social process, 5
Northern Virginia Drug Ring, 10

Pachuco gangs, 27, 51–53, 164. *See also* Sleepy Lagoon case
Penny papers, 35, 81, 111–112
Police beat, 87
Political economy and news production, 63, 77
Primary definers, 108–110, 124
Progressive Movement, 32, 44
Public education and growth of mass media, 35

Rap music and police, 127

Sleepy Lagoon case, 51
Social service organizations, 135, 150–151; resources and funding, 150; and use of local news, 136
Sources: experts, 110; minorities, 140; police, 105
"Sweeps" (TV ratings), 92

Telegraph, 35
Television news: biased, 9; consultants for, 82–83

Villa, Pancho, and newsreels, 43

"Writing White," 85

Yellow journalism, 112
Youth gangs, Mexican American: leadership 102; myths about, 79–80

Zoot-suit riots, 17, 51, 164

About the Author

RAÚL DAMACIO TOVARES is an Assistant Professor in the Department of Communication at Trinity College in Washington, D.C. His areas of study include television news, film, international communication, and ethnic representations in mass media. He has published extensively both in journals and in edited collections.

OHIO UNIVERSITY LIBRARY

Please return this book as soon as you have finished with it. In order to avoid a fine it must be returned by the latest date stamped below. All books are subject to recall after two weeks or immediately if needed for reserve.

CF